HORNBY
magazine yearbook

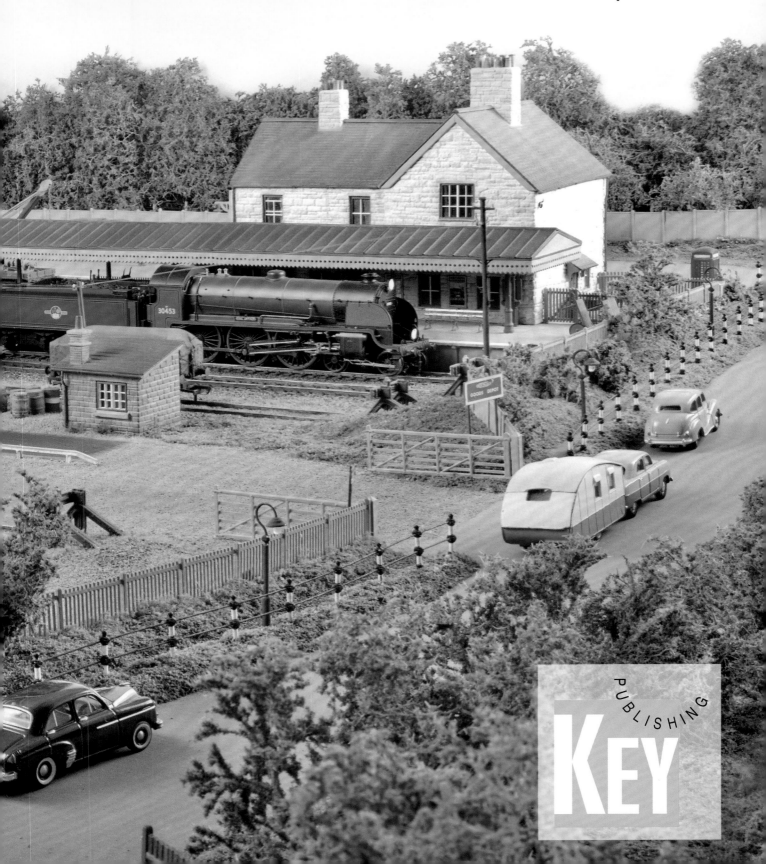

HORNBY
magazine yearbook

Edited by Mike Wild

KEY
PUBLISHING

Editor: Mike Wild
Sub Editor:
Andrew Roden
Design: Ian Blaza
Contributors:
Evan Green Hughes, Paul
Chetter, Nigel Burkin,
Phil Parker and Brian
Stephenson.

First published,
November 2013

ISBN:
978-0-946219-30-8

Printed in England by
Berforts Information
Press Ltd, Southfield
Road, Eynsham, Oxford
OX29 4JB.

Published by:
Key Publishing Ltd,
PO Box 100, Stamford
Lincolnshire PE9 1QX.

Visit the Key Publishing
website at
www.keypublishing.com

CONTENTS

WELC

Take 12 weeks, a part built but barely started model railway and an idea for a Southern Region theme model and what do you get? The answer is Twelve Trees Junction, the project layout for *Hornby Magazine Yearbook No. 6*.

In this sixth Yearbook we're exploring the potential of modelling the Southern Region having followed the Western Region in Yearbook No. 4 and the London Midland Region in Yearbook No. 5.

The project layout for this book has come from the mothballed and previously stored Project 12 which first appeared in *Hornby Magazine* in HM56. A change of office premises meant we didn't have the space to continue building the layout at the time, but now things have moved on and Project 12 is reborn.

It has been an enthralling project to work on. Modelling the Southern, particularly in the 1950s/1960s, is a time intensive process as not only do you have to lay track, add wiring, ballasting and all the other jobs, you also need third-rail

to go with Electric Multiple Units. And we had particular ideas about modelling an urban setting which invariably takes longer to fulfil than a country model.

We reckon the end result is well worth the time and effort and we are now well on the way towards completing this layout for its exhibition debut at the *Hornby Magazine* Great Electric Train Show in 2014 – by then it will measure 32ft x 8ft including its fiddle yards!

Naturally this book is about much more than just the Southern Region. This hobby has so much to offer and each

BR 'Standard Four' 4-6-0 75072 draws away from Twelve Trees Junction with a parcels working. In the bay platform a 2-H DEMU waits for passengers from the recently arrived pair of 2-BILs from London.

OME

year we look back at the big releases of the past 12 months and forward to the coming year. Both are equally exciting, but off the back of the Blue Pullman release in 2012 by Bachmann it was hard to see how that could be topped.

However, as I write this at the start of October, that looks set to happen in just a few weeks time as Hatton's of Liverpool is about to complete production of the LMS Beyer Garratt 2-6-0+0-6-2 – the largest single locomotive model ever to be mass

produced as a ready-to-run item for 'OO' gauge. Does it get any better?

Well, if you are a Southern modeller then the answer to that is more than likely yes as, on August 31, Bachmann announced it would be producing a brand new ready-to-run model of the 'Brighton Atlantic' 4-4-2s for 'OO' gauge for release in 2015.

Railway modelling is full of surprises like these and we revel in discovering the latest news and bringing it to light through the pages of *Hornby Magazine*.

It is a great pleasure to be the editor for this magazine and Yearbook and from all of us here at *Hornby Magazine* we hope you enjoy Yearbook No. 6.
Happy modelling!

Mike Wild

Mike Wild
Editor, Hornby Magazine

Twelve Trees
JUNCTION
CONCEPT AND DESIGN

In January 2012 we launched a new layout project in *Hornby Magazine*, and after an enforced break in construction it is back as the centrepiece for *Hornby Magazine Yearbook No. 6*. **Mike Wild** reveals the concept and design for Twelve Trees Junction and explains how it has adapted and evolved.

It's a dream of many railway modellers: complex track formations with multiple points and crossing, trains changing routes, steam, diesel and electric traction and the ever changing face of British Railways in the late 1950s all set in a bustling, compact urban location.

There was only one area that could fit the bill for this project - British Railways Southern Region. Its combination of steam, diesel and electric traction offers tremendous scope in variety, in operation and appearance. This new layout will become our flagship exhibition layout in 2014 and, for those who remember it, a fitting replacement for Bay Street Shed Mk II.

Twelve Trees Junction is the third theme layout for the Hornby Magazine Yearbook following on from St Stephens Road (HMYB4) with its BR Western Region theme and Topley Dale (HMYB5) with its BR London Midland Region theme.

When we started building this layout the concept was very different, in fact about as different as it could be without being set in the highlands of Scotland at the end of a sleepy branch line. The plan originally called for a double track main line, a sizeable station with a bay platform to serve a branch line, a goods yard and goods loops for both main lines. Quaint country buildings would have surrounded the station in limited numbers while a traditional goods shed would serve the yard.

However, that plan was created almost two years ago now and since Twelve Trees Junction – nicknamed Project 12 – last featured in Hornby Magazine (HM61) it has been in storage awaiting workshop space. Time changes things and having brought the virtually bare baseboards back to our workshop again during summer this year it became clear that our original vision was lacking a certain

something to make it different from our other project layouts.

All of the features, while perfectly fine, were typical of many model railways built by Hornby Magazine. We'd built goods yards before and we'd built country stations and motive power depots before too. What this needed was an altogether different atmosphere.

Southern theme

Having covered the Western and Midland Regions as the main theme in Hornby Magazine Yearbooks No. 4 and No. 5 respectively, this year we decided to head South again, but this time to the South East rather than the South West.

The Southern Region of BR is a popular subject and recent releases of third-rail Electric Multiple Units (EMUs) in 'OO' scale have made it much more possible, and simple, to model the busy routes of BR's smallest region, and the Southern's variety is unparallelled in terms of

The combination of steam, diesel and electric traction makes the Southern Region an attractive proposition. Twelve Trees Junction is set to represent a suburban scene in the 1960s. On July 15 1964 'Merchant Navy' 35012 United States Line approaches Vauxhall, soon after leaving Waterloo, with the 6.30pm to Bournemouth while BR 4-EPB 5332 runs parallel as empty stock. Brian Stephenson.

TWELVE TREES JUNCTION

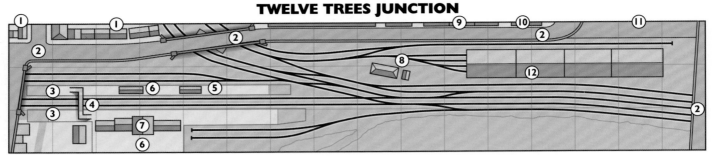

KEY

1. Town Buildings	4. Footbridge	7. Factory	10. Flats
2. Road	5. Station buildings	8. Signal Box	11. Bus depot
3. Platform	6. Station forecourt	9. Tennament buildings	12. Carriage shed

The Southern Region around the London suburbs was filled with junctions and complex point work, which looked even busier due to the live third-rail. BR 4-EPB 5333 leaves Norwood Junction on a Selhurst to Stewarts Lane empty stock move in June 1967. Brian Stephenson.

traction with steam, diesel and electric all running side by side in one of the most densely populated areas in the country.

Our model will be firmly set in 1957-1967, the final decade of steam on the Southern. This provides the opportunity for the widest variety of locomotive classes possible as many of the Maunsell and other pre-Bulleid locomotive designs were still in service until the early 1960s. At the same time multiple units continued to be developed and the period saw the first of BR's standard designs enter traffic alongside pre-nationalisation classes with the final additions during the period being the

4-CIG, 4-BIG and 4-VEP units.

Diesel traction on the Southern was concentrated on a limited number of types including Southern based Classes 33 and 73 plus visiting classes such as the Class 42 'Warships' from the Western and Class 47s from the Eastern and Midland. Other classes did appear in different parts of the Southern Region too but only on an occasional basis.

Taking stock of all the classes available off the shelf it soon becomes clear that it is very feasible to create a representative fleet of locomotives for the Southern from ready-to-run models with the added advantage of Maunsell, Bulleid and

Mk 1 stock already being available and SECR 'Birdcage' carriages soon to be released by Bachmann.

Urban feeling

To move Twelve Trees Junction away from its original country station theme didn't take much persuasion. The name of the layout naturally suggested a junction, but the trackplan didn't feature this important component on scene.

The space available to Twelve Trees Junction is vast compared to our previous layouts with the scenic section measuring 16ft x 3ft. The maximum board width of our previous layouts has

been 2ft 6in, but the extra 6in offered by the boards for Twelve Trees really makes a difference and its length has proved to be an asset too.

Having tried out a number of options for using the space available with spare track components a new arrangement was settled on fairly quickly which would see a substantial double junction in the centre of the layout with the station to one side and the yard to the other.

The roots of the junction – if you'll excuse the pun on the layout's name - came from reading about the 'Quarry Line' route which bypasses Redhill on the Brighton Main Line. The junction on the layout bypasses the station at Twelve Trees to take an alternative route, although its position is much closer to the station throat than any real example known to us.

Having developed the junction theme the goods yard was next for a rethink. Having considered its original position it became clear that its access would no longer work and that big changes were needed. The first change came in the form of a revised connection between the main lines and proposed goods yard sidings resulting in a headshunt operated from the other end of a new inner goods loop.

The next idea was to use the newly arranged goods yard as a set of exchange sidings for oil or cement traffic – ideas prompted by Hornby's then soon to be released Sentinel 4wDM and the planned model of a Fawley oil train for the layout. However, further consideration and posting of a question on the *Hornby Magazine* Facebook page offered a new solution – carriage sidings.

Having built up a substantial fleet of EMUs for Bay Street Shed Mk II some years ago we already had plenty of stock to hand to fill a set of EMU carriage sidings and the idea definitely provided for something different. Having raided the *Hornby Magazine* store for buildings we found a Bachmann carriage shed structure and this set the tone for development of the original goods yard site.

The next step in the layout's evolution was the backdrop. Having decided on an urban theme we wanted to better what had gone before on Bay Street. That layout had two major flaws in its design – firstly the backdrop was lacking in relief and height, and secondly the curved baseboards at each end hid parts of the scenery from view at certain angles.

With this in mind Twelve Trees Junction was already one major step ahead in that it has straight baseboards avoiding the potential for parts of the scenery to be

THE ORIGINAL CONCEPT

The original baseboards have been used for the rejuvenated Twelve Trees Junction, but this is how the first concept began – a country through station with modest facilities.

Following track laying, with Peco code 75, the plan offered a double track main line with passing loops and a goods yard – a simple through station.

The goods yard was designed for interesting operation with a short loop, a kick back siding and a headshunt which disappeared off scene to give maximum space.

The station theme called for an ageing but well kept station building using Bachmann's Sheffield Park buildings together with a modern concrete faced platform.

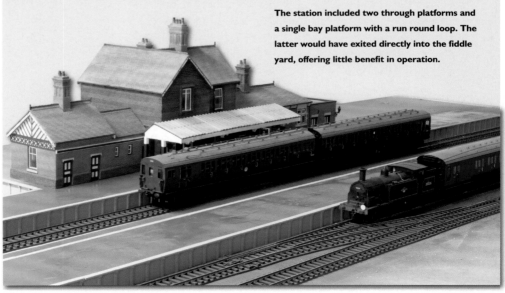

The station included two through platforms and a single bay platform with a run round loop. The latter would have exited directly into the fiddle yard, offering little benefit in operation.

hidden or disjointed. However, it needed to have a consistent feel to it to reflect the idea of an urban setting somewhere on the outskirts of central London such as Thornton Heath, Sydenham or Norwood Junction.

The location of Twelve Trees has enhanced its variety too. Its design is freelance, but is intended to be set close to Norwood Junction, an area which saw a variety of locomotive classes, both steam and diesel, appear from other regions on transfer freights. Strange as it may sound

this includes LMS '8F' 2-8-0s, 'WD' 2-8-0s, BR '9F' 2-10-0s, plus ex-LNER 0-6-0s such as 'J19' and 'J20'. On the diesel front transfer freights were seen on the Southern in the hands of Classes 15, 16, 20, 24, 25, 27 and 31 amongst others.

As with any model, the plan is bound to change as the build progresses, but the full story is here with features on construction of the layout itself including trackwork, buildings, rolling stock, scenery and more.

Fiddle yard design

With a complex track plan such as Twelve Trees building a suitable fiddle yard is a potentially complex task.

The initial idea focused on two options for a fiddle yard – a continuous run

with a large storage yard to the rear in typical fashion for an exhibition layout or a pair of turntable fiddle yards, one positioned at each end of the layout. In either format it would be impossible to set the layout up in our workshop due to its total size, but there were drawbacks with both, and particularly with the final trackplan for the model.

With three exits from the layout the continuous run fiddle yard would have been difficult to service by all routes and, moreover, would have meant at least a 10ft total depth for the model which isn't always suited to exhibition venues. However, the second option of turntable fiddle yards wasn't really practical either as we wanted to be able to run eight coach trains, considerably more than we felt comfortable with turning.

This then left two options, the first of which would be a cassette fiddle yard. Again, operationally we felt this wouldn't have provided the level of train movements we wanted and also meant a lot of handling of the rolling stock.

The final plan draws on inspiration from North American layouts. Twelve Trees will use two return loop fiddle yards. At the carriage sidings end of the layout this is a simple addition as the exit and entry tracks simply link together without any concerns. Storage loops will be laid on the fiddle yards for additional train space, but the station end of the layout with its junction will require at least two reverse loop modules to cope with changing over the power supply polarity to work with the double junction.

Once the fiddle yards are built (a job planned for early 2014) Twelve Trees Junction will be in the region of 32ft long as each fiddle yard is planned to cover an 8ft x 8ft area to provide plenty of space for train storage.

Twelve Trees Junction represents the most ambitious and exciting *Hornby Magazine* layout project to date. Keep reading to find out how we developed the bare baseboards into the fully scenic model you see on the cover…

USEFUL LINKS

www.southernregion.net
www.semgonline.com
www.southernelectric.org.uk

The appearance of other region'=s locomotives was rare on the Southern, but around London numerous different steam and diesel classes from the Midland and Eastern Regions appeared on transfer freights across the capital. At the head of a Willesden Junction to Norwood Junction transfer freight, ex-LMS '8F' 2-8-0 48247 passes Crystal Palace (low level) in August 1962.
Brian Stephenson.

TWELVE TREES JUNCTION

BASEBOARDS
track and third-rail

Unsatisfied with the original trackplan for Twelve Trees Junction, **Mike Wild** set about redeveloping it to create the new suburban London theme.

I t just wasn't inspirational. After more than a year in storage what lay before us as the basis for Twelve Trees Junction was bare, barren and empty. This was perhaps expected as the layout literally consisted of baseboards with only a modest track layout and the platforms to give it any relief.

The original plan was sound, but the more we looked at it the more we felt we could do more with the expansive 16ft x 3ft footprint of the scenic area – and besides, if it was to be called Twelve Trees Junction as planned, it really needed a junction.

The baseboards follow *Hornby Magazine*'s standard designs, only in this case they are wider. The frames are made from 69mm x 18mm planed timber while the tops are 9mm plywood. Two of the four boards are traditional solid top boards which have plywood over their full 4ft x 3ft while the second pair are the same overall size, but have open frames either side of a 2ft wide trackbed to allow scenery to drop below the level of the railway. There is only a modest 30mm height change, but it is enough

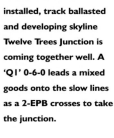

With the third rail installed, track ballasted and developing skyline Twelve Trees Junction is coming together well. A 'Q1' 0-6-0 leads a mixed goods onto the slow lines as a 2-EPB crosses to take the junction.

to make a difference.

The boards are screwed and glued together. They were built back in January 2012, but even after a long period in store the boards were in perfect condition when we returned them to the workshop for continuation of the build.

Modified trackplan

The trackplan has been almost completely replaced with only hints of the original in the final arrangement. Those remnants include the double track main line through the station and the former goods lines, albeit with modified crossings.

The first modification was to consider the impact of adding a diamond crossing to form a double junction in the centre of the layout, in similar vein to that on Bay Street Shed Mk II. However, rather than designing this layout on paper, spare points and crossing were used to mock up a potential arrangement before the final components were ordered to create the end result.

Having tested the idea of a crossing it became clear that in order

WHAT WE USED

Product	Manufacturer	Cat No.
Code 75 Large radius left-hand point	www.peco-uk.com	SL-E189
Code 75 Large radius right-hand point	www.peco-uk.com	SL-E188
Code 75 Medium radius left-hand point	www.peco-uk.com	SL-E196
Code 75 Medium radius right-hand point	www.peco-uk.com	SL-E195
Code 75 Large radius diamond crossing	www.peco-uk.com	SL-194
Code 75 flexible track	www.peco-uk.com	SL-100F
Code 75 metal rail joiners	www.peco-uk.com	SL-110
Code 75 insulated rail joiners	www.peco-uk.com	SL-111
Track pins	www.peco-uk.com	ST-280
1/16thin cork	www.javis.co.uk	JCS116S
Rail built buffer stops	www.peco-uk.com	SL-40
Code 60 Individulay rail	www.peco-uk.com	IL-1
SR third-rail insulator pots	www.peco-uk.com	IL-60
'Z' gauge rail joiners	www.peco-uk.com	SL-210
Medium grade grey blend ballast	www.bachmann.co.uk	B1394
Fine grade grey blend ballast	www.bachmann.co.uk	B1393
Matt No 29 aerosol	www.humbrol.com	29
Matt No 67 aerosol	www.humbrol.com	67

to keep the two goods loops – which would become the Up and Down slow lines heading towards the capital – they needed to be moved too. All this left the station looking rather empty with just a pair of terminus sidings and two through lines.

One idea which had been bubbling during the early stages of the layout's life was to add a second bay platform nearer to the front of the model, and in the end we decided to add two tracks here, but with only one serving a platform face.

The original bay platform and run-round loop to the far side of the station were lifted completely and relaid as a pair of loops which then use a second diamond crossing to rejoin the main line. The end result of this is a complex but attractive junction which certainly sets this layout apart.

A number of adjustments were made to the plan before committing to track laying and the carriage sidings were also mocked up at an early stage to ensure that they would fit as planned.

All of the track on Twelve Trees

Junction is from the Peco code 75 range consisting of large radius points on the main line together with medium radius points in the bay platform and carriage sidings. The final additions are a pair of diamond crossings.

The whole layout has been built with digital control in mind as that is what it will use on completion. Using lessons learned from building Bolsover and Seven Lane Pit and also converting St Stephens Road (HM Yearbook No. 4) to digital we have been able to better plan for the control system and increase operational flexibility.

The entire layout is live and we have ensured that all loops are permanently powered by adding dropper wires to connect to the main feeds. This means that locomotives and units with sound and/or lights won't be disrupted by point changes, offering a more realistic operation at the end of construction. To simplify the wiring though, only one side of each loop needed additional wiring as the outer rail in each case is permanently fed from the point.

A main power bus will run the length of the layout connecting to copper-clad strips glued underneath the boards to provide the power feeds to the track. This method will reduce the amount of wire needed and also help keep the underside of the boards neater and more organised.

The diamond crossings for Twelve Trees posed some questions initially as we ideally wanted to use live frog crossings. However, having considered the wiring implications we decided to use insulated frog diamond crossings to reduce the necessary wiring as much as possible. In any case, all of the locomotives and multiple units for Twelve Trees feature multiple pick-ups so we don't expect to have any problems with the trains stalling.

Enter the trackgang

As with many of *Hornby Magazine's* project layouts, Twelve Trees Junction was built to a deadline. From start to finish we had just 10 weeks to build the whole layout from the point of returning

Multiple units are a key component of this model. A 4-CEP enters the freshly ballasted station under the yet to be completed signal gantry.

Step 1 The first step is to mark up the timber battens to make up the baseboard frame. To fit with the 1,200mm x 900mm plywood tops each board requires two lengths of 69mm x 20mm timber cut to 1,200mm plus four 860mm long to make the ends and cross braces. Use a tri-square for accurate 90 degree marks.

Step 2 We process the materials for the baseboard in batches to save a little time in tool handling. This stack of timber is all marked up and ready to cut to form the baseboard frames. After marking each length its dimensions are recorded on the batten as a reminder to what its purpose is.

Step 3 If you have a number of baseboards to build an electric jigsaw is a worthwhile investment as it will save a considerable amount of time and energy in cutting timber.

Step 4 After cutting the timber to form the frame the components for each baseboard were laid out together for a dry run to ensure it would all work as planned. This is the frame which will offer a 4ft x 3ft (1,200mm x 900mm) baseboard – two of these are needed for Twelve Trees.

Step 5 Positioning the 9mm plywood top onto the frame allows final checks to be made before the frame is fixed together permanently.

Step 7 Having carefully positioned the first side timber under the plywood top it can be screwed in place. We use an electric screw driver and 3.5x30mm wood screws to fix the baseboard surface in place. The type of screws used don't require countersunk holes making them quicker to work with.

Step 8 The outer frame is now complete in this view with all four sides glued and screwed to the baseboard top.

Step 6 To assemble the frame start with one of the long sides. Run a bead of PVA glue along its top edge and then position it under the baseboard top. Other timbers from the baseboard frame are useful to support the plywood top during the early stages of construction.

STEP-BY-STEP | BUILDING TWELVE TREES JUNCTION'S BASEBOARDS

Step 9 The cross braces now need to be added to the frame to support the middle of the baseboard surface. Without these the surface would sag in the middle over time. Use a tri-square to position the cross member accurately.

Step 10 Like the outer frame the cross braces are glued and screwed in place. A bead of PVA along the top edge and ends helps secure the cross brace in place. Add screws at both ends through the timber sides and through the baseboard surface for a rigid structure.

Step 11 This is the first of the completed baseboards viewed upside down. Following completion we set this board aside overnight to allow the glue to dry thoroughly and built the second solid top baseboard to the same pattern.

Step 13 The frames for the second pair of boards support a 2ft wide section of plywood on 94mm deep supports which are in turn screwed onto the full width cross braces from 69mm deep timber.

Step 12 To build the open frame baseboards for the rest of the scenic section a similar method has been employed. The sides are 1,200mm long lengths of 69mm x 20mm timber with three cross braces cut to 860mm plus one 860mm length of 94mm x 20mm timber to form the join with the solid top baseboards.

Step 15 With all the timber work complete the baseboards can now be joined together. The first baseboard is supported on two trestle legs with the next three boards requiring one trestle each. For alignment each board is clamped together with G-clamps before bolt holes are drilled through the ends.

Step 14 The baseboard frame is screwed and glued together as per the solid top boards, but this time the frame has to be built independently of the top surface. Use a tri-square for alignment and fix in place with 4.0x40mm wood screws.

Step 16 Three 6mm diameter holes are drilled through to join each baseboard together. 60mm roof bolts are then pushed through with 30mm washers to spread their load. On the rear face wing nuts secure the two boards together.

it to our workshop.

Having established the new trackplan we moved quickly into the tracklaying stage. The first part of the process was to remove pretty much all of the original track except for the main lines through the platforms. With this done, tracklaying started at the main double junction and progressed through the rest of the layout.

The track is laid on 1/16in cork sheet which is then trimmed back to the sleeper ends to create a ballast shoulder during scenic treatment. All of the joints have been made as neat as possible by cutting away the chairs from the top of the end sleeper on lengths of flexible track so that joiners can be slid onto the rail ends between the top of the sleeper and the bottom of the rail. During tracklaying 8mm holes were drilled underneath the centre of each point to prepare for later installation of point motors.

Further detailing of the track focused on preparing for the baseboard joints. As this is a portable exhibition layout we had to ensure that every track end was protected during transit which has involved cutting away between two and three sleepers at each baseboard joint for replacement with copper-clad sleepers. These are pinned to the baseboard, grooved in the centre on

both sides to stop electrical shorts, because we used double-sided copper-clad sleepers, and then soldered to the rails. After soldering the rails can be cut in line with the baseboard joint leaving solid fixing points for the rails.

The double track line which runs at an angle across one of the baseboard joints was more complex, but rather than add copper-clad sleepers at an angle to the tracks we added three or four sleeper width lengths and then cut through them at the same time as cutting the track. The end result is a neat, strong and long lasting track joint which doesn't look out of place at all.

Having done all of this the wiring connections were then added to the layout. Dropper wires were added at every position where feeds were required and fed through the baseboard. Initially these weren't connected, but later the droppers were soldered onto copper-clad strips which were, in turn, then connected to the power bus which runs the length of the layout to supply power to the track.

The final phase of the tracklaying process was weathering. For this the entire layout was cleared of buildings, rolling stock and vehicles so that the track could be weathered with spray paint. This method requires preparation, but the actual painting takes just a few

minutes. Importantly though, all of the point blades were masked with Tamiya masking tape to keep the paint from entering the electrical contacts of the points.

With this done Humbrol Matt 29 and Matt 67 were sprayed over the entire track formation ensuring even coverage of the rail sides and sleepers to create an overall effect. The Matt 67 was misted in over the Matt 29 main colour to add a little difference of shade in the track colouring.

Once complete the masking tape was removed and all the track cleaned meaning that Twelve Trees Junction was ready for the next phase of work.

Third-rail installation

Any Southern Region layout set to feature Electric Multiple Units (EMUs) needs one important component – the third-rail. Twelve Trees Junction is no exception and we have used Peco's Individulay third-rail insulator pots, code 60 rail and 'Z' gauge rail joiners for this model.

Through experience we quickly learned that it is easier to ballast a layout before adding third rail as the extra rail tends to get in the way of tamping ballast into place. So after adding a couple of yards of third-rail we then decided to progress the layout by

Following modifications to the trackplan a new bay platform was added at the front of the layout. An 'M7' stands next to a Class 205 in the new platform.

TOOLS – TRACK LAYING
Minidrill with cutting disc/
hacksaw/specialist track
cutter, pin hammer, pin vice,
1mm drill bit, pliers, electric
drill and 8mm drill bit

STEP-BY-STEP LAYING OUT THE TRACK FOR TWELVE TREES JUNCTION

Step 1 The original track layout from Project 12, re-titled Twelve Trees Junction, left a lot to be desired in terms of operation. This is what we started with after retrieving the layout from storage.

Step 2 One of the first ideas was to add a bay platform and storage siding at the front of the station. A Class 205 sits on the loose laid track to test its look.

Step 3 Using spare track components a new junction arrangement was mocked up over the original track formation. In the background the new carriage sidings are under development too.

Step 4 Various configurations were tried out during this phase of the build before settling on the final arrangement for the junction, which was still modified further after this view!

Step 5 The first area to be adjusted was the crossover in the station. This was moved from being central between the platforms to the end of the platforms. The first of the diamond crossings can be seen behind too.

Step 6 The majority of the original trackplan was removed from the baseboard to allow relaying work to progress. Fortunately it was only pinned down making removal simple and quick.

Step 7 With the old formation out, the new junction pointwork was assembled and positioned on the layout. This being the key area for the whole trackplan, everything else was laid out from this point in each direction.

Step 8 Having assembled the complete junction the layout is taking shape. The new bay platform is also fully connected while the original bay platform and loop at the back of the station is now a pair of through lines.

Step 9 Clearances through the carriage shed are tight as we wanted four tracks through the building. To ensure that the outer tracks were laid straight we used a section of straight planed timber for alignment.

Step 10 Four tracks will just fit through the Bachmann Scenecraft carriage shed buildings used on the layout and offer a perfect fit for Ratio carriage cleaning platforms.

Step 11 With the track in position the next task was to add copperclad sleepers at every baseboard joint. Pieces of copperclad strip were cut to length to match the width of the Peco code 75 sleepers, two pin holes were drilled (one in each end of the sleeper) and the copper surface cut to stop electrical shorts. Each piece of copperclad strip was then pinned to the baseboard before the rails were soldered to it.

Step 12 Next the wire droppers were added wherever they were needed. As this layout is DCC controlled it only needs one pair of colours for power feeds – blue for inner rails, yellow for outer rails. These will later to be connected to the power bus.

Step 13 Weathering of the rails and sleepers commenced next after all the wiring had been finished and tested. The layout was cleared of all stock and buildings and all of the point blades were masked with Tamiya 10mm making tape. Humbrol Matt No 29 and Matt 67 were then sprayed onto the track to give it its final look, for the time being.

ballasting all of the trackwork.

This was achieved using Woodland Scenics fine and medium grade grey blend ballasts which were mixed together before being spread over the track and then brushed into place. Covering such a large area with ballast meant we needed a quick method for fixing it in place. This came in the form of spraying the fresh ballast with water with a drop of detergent added to remove its surface tension followed by a liberal application of 50:50 PVA glue and water mixed together in a washing up liquid bottle.

This is a very rapid way to glue ballast down, but it can also be messy! Some of the ballast will move during the process no matter how wet it is, but small areas can be attended to at a later point to refine the finished look of the ballast.

Having left the ballast to dry thoroughly overnight attention returned to third-rail installation. The code 60 rail is supplied in 2ft lengths. Each 2ft length requires 17 insulator pots which also means drilling 17 1mm diameter holes in the ends of sleepers. To speed the process along we used an electric minidrill to make the holes in every fifth sleeper – the correct spacing for

Southern Railway/Region third-rail. Some compromises were made around pointwork to ensure the third-rail was stable.

For a more realistic finish we used 'Z' gauge rail joiners to join lengths of code 60 rail together meaning that full baseboards could have a single length of third-rail on each running line – another improvement that we made to our methods after first installing third-rail on Bay Street Mk II (Yearbook No 2). The most complicated area of third-rail installation is around points. Having consulted BR diagrams we moved

forward stage by stage around points to ensure that, as much as possible, our arrangement followed that set out by the real railway. It is a long process, but well worth the effort.

Having completed all of the third-rail installation we had a good looking railway, but one in need of weathering to tone down the shiny rails and bright ballast. That though was held for another day while we pressed on with scenic work on Twelve Trees Junction…

■ **Turn to page 86 for the next instalment on Twelve Trees Junction.**

The Southern Region featured multi-track main lines, particularly on the approaches to the capital. This section of Twelve Trees Junction sets out to recreate some of that atmosphere.

STEP-BY-STEP | BALLASTING TWELVE TREES JUNCTION

Step 1 To begin the ballasting process Woodland Scenics fine and medium grade grey blend ballasts were mixed together and then sprinkled over the track formation.

Step 2 Next the loose ballast was brushed into place with a 3/4in paint brush, taking care to ensure it all sat neatly between the sleepers and either side of each running line.

Step 3 Once all the ballast was brushed into place it looks like this. After doing this area we decided to hold off on installing any more third-rail until ballasting was complete.

Step 4 To keep the point blades free from glue we ran a little gear oil between the blades and on the mechanism. This stops the PVA/water mix from contaminating these areas.

Step 5 The ballast was then wetted using a plant water mister filled with cold water and a drop of detergent to remove the water's surface tension allowing it to flow more easily into the ballast.

Step 6 PVA wood glue was mixed to a 50:50 ratio with water and loaded into an old washing up liquid bottle. This was then used to apply the glue to the ballast. This method is quick, but does look messy. Once dried though it will look much better…

The SOUTHERN survey

Ready-to-run models are continually appearing and disappearing. **Mike Wild** surveys the range of Southern Region steam and diesel locomotives and multiple units that have been produced in 'OO' gauge to suit the BR steam era.

The Southern was different - different to all the other BR regions. The original purpose of the wider railway network was for the transport of goods, and particularly minerals, but on the Southern the passenger was king.

From the early 1900s the network, which ultimately became the Southern Railway in 1923 and later BR's Southern Region, has kept the movement of passengers at the forefront of its thinking, and it is the same story today.

Electric units were introduced early with the first arriving on the London, Brighton and South Coast Railway in 1909, but later the third-rail electrification scheme was introduced which spread across the region to become one of it's signatures.

However, as much as Electric Multiple Units (EMUs) are synonymous with the Southern it had many other features. Perhaps one of the most notable is the name Bulleid. Chief Mechanical Engineer to the Southern Railway from 1937-1949, Bulleid's steam locomotive designs offered something unique, fresh and

different to the other regions. While the Great Western and London Midland & Scottish railways continued in standard fashions (as did the London and North Eastern Railway when funds allowed), Bulleid developed his outstanding air-smoothed 'Pacifics', the delightful – or ugly depending on how you look at it – 'Q1' 0-6-0 and the ill-fated 'Leader'.

These designs were backed up by hard working creations from his predecessor Richard Maunsell as well as a wide range of pre-grouping locomotive designs bringing the chance to see an early 1900s South Eastern and Chatham Railway (SECR) 0-6-0 running alongside 'modern' diesel classes such as the BRCW Class 33s and BR's first generation Electric Multiple Units.

READY-TO-RUN SOUTHERN STEAM, 'OO' GAUGE

Class	Manufacturer	Availability
Bulleid 'Q1' 0-6-0	Hornby	Current
Bulleid air-smoothed 'West Country' 4-6-2	Hornby	Due 2014
Bulleid rebuilt 'West Country' 4-6-2	Hornby	Current
Bulleid rebuilt 'Merchant Navy' 4-6-2	Hornby	Current
Maunsell 'N' 2-6-0	Bachmann	Current
Maunsell 'Lord Nelson' 4-6-0	Bachmann	Ex-catalogue
Maunsell 'King Arthur' 4-6-0	Hornby	Due 2014
Maunsell 'Schools' 4-4-0	Hornby	Due 2014
Stroudley 'Terrier' 0-6-0T	Hornby	Current
Drummond 'M7' 0-4-4T	Hornby	Current
Drummond 'T9' 4-4-0	Hornby	Due 2014
Beattie '0298' 2-4-0WT	Kernow MRC	Current
Adams 'O2' 0-4-4T	Kernow MRC	Due 2014
Wainwright 'C' 0-6-0	Bachmann	Current
Billinton 'E4' 0-6-2T	Bachmann	Due 2014
Billinton 'H2' 4-4-2	Bachmann	Due 2015
Wainwright 'H' 0-4-4T	OO Works	Ex-catalogue
Drummond '700' 0-6-0	OO Works	Ex-catalogue
LMS Fairburn 2-6-4T	Bachmann	Current
BR 'Britannia' 4-6-2	Hornby	Current
BR '5MT' 4-6-0	Bachmann	Current
BR '4MT' 4-6-0	Hornby	Current
BR '4MT' 4-6-0	Bachmann	Current
BR '4MT' 2-6-0	Bachmann	Current
BR '4MT' 2-6-4T	Bachmann	Current
BR '3MT' 2-6-2T	Bachmann	Current

Above: Rebuilt 'Battle of Britain' 4-6-2 34052 *Lord Dowding* departs London Waterloo with the 6.00pm to Salisbury as BR '4MT' 2-6-4T 80012 approaches with empty coaching stock on August 26 1966. Brian Stephenson.

Left: BR '5MT' 4-6-0 73089 leads the 6.09pm London Waterloo to Basingstoke through Clapham Junction on August 16 1966. Brian Stephenson.

The variety of the Southern –
whether Railway or Region - is perhaps
one of the reasons that so many ready-
to-run models have been produced in
recent years. The pace of investment
hasn't stopped either with Bachmann
announcing the Billinton 'H2' class
'Atlantic' for 'OO' gauge at the end of
August 2013. This brand new model
fills a significant gap in ready-to-run
products as none of the British 4-4-2s
have ever been produced until now.

Steam power

By far the leader when it comes
to Southern steam is Hornby. The
manufacturer relaunched itself in
the 1990s when it issued its brand
new model of the Bulleid rebuilt
'Merchant Navy' 4-6-2. Since then it
has accelerated through a programme
of development which has seen
high quality ready-to-run models of
the air-smoothed and rebuilt 'West
Country'/'Battle of Britain' 4-6-2s,
Bulleid 'Q1' 0-6-0s, Maunsell 'King

READY-TO-RUN SOUTHERN EMU/DEMUS, 'OO' GAUGE

Class	Manufacturer	Availability
2-BIL, two-car EMU	Hornby	Current
5-BEL, five-car Pullman EMU	Hornby	Current
2-EPB, two-car EMU	Bachmann	Current
2-H, two-car DEMU	Kernow MRC	Current
4-CEP, four-car EMU	Bachmann	Current
4-VEP, four-car EMU	Hornby	Current
MLV, motorised luggage van	Bachmann	Current

READY-TO-RUN SOUTHERN DIESEL AND ELECTRIC, 'OO' GAUGE

Class	Manufacturer	Availability
LMS 10000/10001	Bachmann	Current
Bulleid 10201-10203	Kernow MRC	Due 2014
BR Class 08	Hornby	Current
BR Class 08	Bachmann	Current
BR Class 09	Hornby	Ex-catalogue
BR Class 33	Heljan	Current
BR Class 42 (Western Region)	Bachmann	Current
BR Class 47	Bachmann	Current
BR Class 73	Hornby	Current
BR Class 73	Dapol	Due 2013

Arthur' 4-6-0, Drummond 'M7' 0-4-4T and 'T9' 4-4-0 and even a 21st Century standard model of the Maunsell 'Schools' 4-4-0 hit the shelves.

For a long time Bachmann's Southern steam range has been comparatively limited with just the Maunsell 'N' 2-6-0 and the impressive Maunsell 'Lord Nelson' 4-6-0 in its armoury.

However, in recent times it has begun growing a range of the rather more elegant pre-nationalisation locomotive designs which operated on the Southern with the first being the SECR 'C' class 0-6-0. The latest announcements by Bachmann are the Billinton 'E4' 0-6-2T and the Billinton 'H2' 4-4-2 which are due for release in 2014 and 2015 respectively.

While Bachmann and Hornby hold the majority of the Southern Region steam designs, there are two other manufacturers with a penchant for the

Drummond '700' and Wainwright 'H' 0-4-4T. These models are highly sought after and are now only available second-hand.

However, it wasn't just the Southern's locomotives which worked on the region. In the early 1950s problems with the 'Merchant Navy' fleet saw ex-LNER 'V2' 2-6-2s and 'B1' 4-6-0s drafted in and these two classes were temporarily allocated to Southern Region depots.

Also seen on the Southern were the Fairburn 2-6-4Ts. 41 were built at Brighton Works for the Southern Region using the LMS design to replace older designs, many of these engines worked out their careers on the Southern.

Transfer freights between London's

2-6-4T plus the '3MT' 2-6-2T to complete the picture. The Standards became much more common on the region in the final years of steam following mass withdrawals of pre-nationalisation and pre-grouping classes in the early 1960s.

Diesels and electrics

With the onset of electrification on the Southern, the use of diesel locomotives was relatively limited with a handful of specific classes which were rarely seen off region.

The earliest of these were Bulleid's 1-Co-Co-1 diesels 10201-10203 which entered traffic in 1950-1954 and during 1953-1955 they were joined by LMS pioneer diesels 10000 and 10001 for further trials.

The 1955 Modernisation plan brought with it new locomotives for the Southern including the Class 71 Bo-Bo electrics, which are yet to be produced as ready-to-run locomotive, the Class 73 Bo-Bo electro-diesels and the BRCW built Class 33 diesels. The Class 73 is represented by the longstanding model from the Lima stable which is now produced by Hornby, although Dapol is currently finalising a brand new production of the iconic Southern electro-diesel. The diminutive Class 09 diesel shunter (the latter largely based on the Southern Region) is available from Hornby and Bachmann.

Below left: Drummond 'M7' 0-4-4T 30670 departs Exeter St Davids with a local goods for Exeter Central on August 13 1956. Bob Tuck/Rail Archive Stephenson.

Below right: As well as its fleet of EMUs the Southern Region boasted a unique fleet of Diesel Electric Multiple Units. Hampshire DEMU 1115 arrives at Alresford on a Southampton to Alton service on November 3 1963. Mike Fox/Rail Archive Stephenson.

> "By far the leader when it comes to Southern steam is Hornby. The manufacturer relaunched itself in the 1990s when it issued its band new model of the Bulleid 'Merchant Navy'."

era – Kernow Model Rail Centre and OO Works.

Kernow Model Rail Centre has commissioned a substantial number of exclusive models and the first to arrive was the Beattie '0298' 2-4-0WT in 2012. Since that model's launch Kernow has commissioned a second steam locomotive in the Adams 'O2' 0-4-4T which is expected to become available in 2014.

OO Works was an early proponent of the Southern steam locomotive producing short runs of handbuilt models. Its back catalogue includes the 'King Arthur', 'L' 4-4-0, 'E4' 0-6-2T,

impressive collection of marshalling yards also brought a wide variety of locomotive classes onto the Southern. Contemporary reports reveal that Stanier '8F' and 'WD' 2-8-0s were both seen together with BR '9F' 2-10-0s and even LNER 'J19' and 'J20' 0-6-0s.

A model of the Southern Region in the 1950s and 1960s wouldn't be complete without the BR Standard steam designs and, happily, an almost full complement of suitable locomotives for the area is available in ready-to-run form in 'OO' gauge. Modellers have the choice of a 'Britannia' 4-6-2, '5MT' and '4MT' 4-6-0s, the '4MT' 2-6-0 and the '4MT'

The Class 33 meanwhile is represented by Heljan in all three forms covering standard, push-pull fitted and narrow bodied variants. Hornby also produces a Class 33 in its RailRoad range.

While the Southern's own fleet of diesels may be limited a wide range of other classes appeared, particularly around London on transfer freights. Here classes 15, 16, 20, 24, 25, 27 and 52 were all seen. In addition the Brush Class 47s were regular performers on the Southern while the Western Region's 'Warship' hydraulics became regular performers on London Waterloo-Exeter workings in the 1960s. All of these classes are now available ready-to-run.

Multiple units

An unexpected and welcome change came when Bachmann announced its plans to produce a ready-to-run model of the BR 4-CEP EMU in July 2006 which has opened up a whole new market for Southern Region EMU models.

Today we have a choice of BR first generation units from Bachmann covering the 4-CEP, 2-EPB and MLV while Hornby has stepped into the fray with models of the 4-VEP alongside the 5-BEL 'Brighton Belle' units and, most recently, the 2-BIL EMU. Added to this Kernow Model Rail Centre launched its Class 205 DEMU this year.

Several versions of each ready-to-run

READY-TO-RUN SOUTHERN LOCOMOTIVES AND MULTIPLE UNITS, 'N' GAUGE

Class	Manufacturer	Availability
Stroudley 'Terrier' 0-6-0T	Dapol	Due 2013
Maunsell 'Schools' 4-4-0	Dapol	Due 2014
Maunsell 'N' 2-6-0	Farish	Due 2014
Bulleid air-smoothed 'West Country' 4-6-2	Dapol	Due 2014
Bulleid rebuilt 'West Country' 4-6-2	Dapol	Due 2014
Bulleid air-smoothed 'Merchant Navy' 4-6-2	Farish	Due 2014
Bulleid 'Q1' 0-6-0	Dapol	Current
LMS Fairburn 2-6-4T	Farish	Due 2013
BR 'Britannia' 4-6-2	Dapol	Current
BR '5MT' 4-6-0	Farish	Current
BR '4MT' 2-6-0	Farish	Current
BR '4MT' 2-6-4T	Farish	Due 2014
BR '3MT' 2-6-2T	Farish	Current
Class 08	Farish	Current
Class 33	Dapol	Due 2014
Class 42	Farish	Current
Class 47	Farish	Current
Class 73	Dapol	Ex-catalogue
4-CEP, four-car EMU	Farish	Current
5-BEL, five-car Pullman EMU	Hornby	Due 2014

EMU have now been released with the Hornby 2-BIL being such a success that a second batch was ordered immediately for release towards the end of 2013.

This shift change in practice has opened up a new world of potential of Southern Region modellers and combined with the impressive range of kits available from DC Kits, No Nonsense Kits (now through Phoenix Precision Paints), Southern Pride, Marc Models, Roxey Mouldings and others.

Passenger stock

Like locomotives the range of carriages available to the Southern modeller is expanding too. Two new carriage types are in production at present with Bachmann working on the SECR 'Birdcage' bogie stock with vehicles to form correct formations, and Kernow Model Rail Centre developing its LSWR 'Gate Stock' push-pull sets to run with its Adams 'O2' 0-4-4T.

Three other main types of passenger stock are available with Bachmann producing the Bulleid corridor stock with a choice of three different vehicles and the BR Mk 1 stock in Southern Region green. In the later design a wide range of different vehicles are available including the BSK and BCK brakes, opens, corridors, restaurant and buffet stock.

Hornby meanwhile has concentrated its efforts on the Maunsell corridor stock with both low and high window side corridor carriages being produced. These have now been released in

Southern Railway olive and malachite green liveries as well as BR carmine and cream and BR green.

In more recent times Hornby has begun adding further vehicle types to its Maunsell collection including the 1960s converted push-pull sets and solo models of the Open Second in both Southern Railway and Southern Region green liveries.

Overview

The Southern Region may have been the smallest on BR in terms of square miles, but its operations were extensive and varied. The vast range of products available ready-to-run shows its popularity and even today new Southern layouts continue to appear fresh on the exhibition circuit.

Here at *Hornby Magazine* we've always had a soft spot for the Southern and the project to build Twelve Trees Junction has shown just how far the availability of suitable rolling stock has come since we retired Bay Street Shed two years ago. If you model the Southern then you are spoilt for choice, particularly with Bachmann's recent announcement of the Billinton 'H2' 4-4-2 for 'OO' too. However, the potential of this region isn't confined to 'OO' gauge. 'N' gauge too has a growing range of products for the region – see Table 5 – while 'O' gauge has also begun to develop a small following for the Southern through Dapol's planned new models of the 'Terrier' 0-6-0T, six-wheel milk tanker and SR 'Pillbox' brake van. ■

DCC
THROTTLE SELECTION

Not all DCC systems are the same and the choice of a system may be affected by factors as simple as the look and feel of the controllers. **Nigel Burkin** sheds more light on the subject.

I am often asked which Digital Command Control (DCC) system I recommend when I'm exhibiting a layout at a show. That is an awkward one to answer because there are many systems available today, all loaded with many different features. Choosing a digital system is very personal and my own preferences might not meet the needs of the next modeller.

The wide choice of systems can be overwhelming and the quoted numbers too. In reality, being able to select from 9,999 addresses, control something along the lines of 40 locomotives simultaneously and be able to hook up to 16 handsets or controllers at once might be more than enough for most of us. When it comes to the numbers, the key one is power; normally around 5amps for a standard system and between eight

and ten amps for a heavy duty system designed for use with large scale layouts where current draw is likely to be higher.

With this in mind, a choice of digital system should not necessarily be made upon the numbers (unless your layout project is truly ambitious in size) but how much current you are likely to need and how you are going to work with the digital system. However, of all the components that make up a digital system - command station, power station, transformer and controller - the most important one is the controller. That is the device you will use to drive trains, the one you will develop a relationship with, so choose carefully!

Realistic operation

One of the benefits of DCC is being able to drive trains in a more realistic

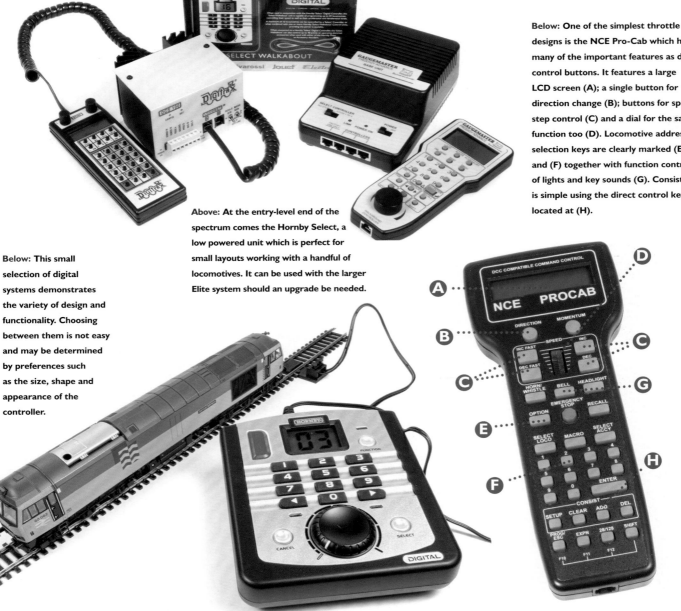

Above: At the entry-level end of the spectrum comes the Hornby Select, a low powered unit which is perfect for small layouts working with a handful of locomotives. It can be used with the larger Elite system should an upgrade be needed.

Below: This small selection of digital systems demonstrates the variety of design and functionality. Choosing between them is not easy and may be determined by preferences such as the size, shape and appearance of the controller.

Below: One of the simplest throttle designs is the NCE Pro-Cab which has many of the important features as direct control buttons. It features a large LCD screen (A); a single button for direction change (B); buttons for speed step control (C) and a dial for the same function too (D). Locomotive address selection keys are clearly marked (E) and (F) together with function control of lights and key sounds (G). Consisting is simple using the direct control keys located at (H).

manner than is possible with analogue control. Real railways do not throw section switches to provide power to a locomotive and isolate others to avoid operational conflicts, so why should that be considered the norm for model railway operation?

DCC provides a realistic driving experience by providing constant power to the layout so each locomotive and multiple unit is in contact with power from which it can draw current for the motor, lights, sound and smoke units. The track current is rectified and controlled by a locomotive decoder which can be allocated its own unique identity. All of these features are controlled by the modeller using the controller or throttle.

The reason why a DCC controller is called a 'throttle' (or sometimes 'cab') is because it replicates the controls found in the cab of a full size locomotive. The throttle is used to drive trains including changes in speed, direction and full independent control of running lights and sound too, if installed. When a modeller selects a locomotive address, full independent control of that locomotive is acquired no matter what other operators are doing, unless you are trying to 'steal' another's locomotive!

As function buttons are pressed, signals are sent to the command station via a four or six wire cable called a throttle or controller bus which is separate from the track power supply bus. The command station interprets the information from the controller and then sends instructions as digital packets through to the layout track, boosted by the power station to track voltage. The decoder picks up the digital packets assigned to its address and responds accordingly. Remaining locomotives on the layout will ignore those particular instructions because the address targeted by the throttle will not be assigned to them.

DCC standards

There are two sides to digital systems from a standards point of view. The command station to track element, and the controller side of the system. The first is governed by an accepted set of standards that ensures all digital decoders and devices will work with any digital system. It even specifies the colour and use of decoder wires or the functions of the pins in a plug and play decoder. It's a feature that means you can run any digital engine on any digital

'DCC puts you in the cab', so goes the saying! The design of most DCC controllers provides the basic driving controls you will find in a steam or diesel locomotive. The controls of a Class 37 are shown to advantage in this view, including the brake, reversing lever and power handle. This explains why so many modellers call DCC controllers a 'cab' or 'throttle'.

Above: The beauty of radio or infrared control is the freedom to operate and watch trains from any location of a layout. The author's Folkestone east project is being built on the third deck of a multi-level layout where radio has been found to be advantageous over tethered throttles.

Right: Another console system with command station, booster and controller in one box is the Digitrax Zephyr (Xtra). It is a feature rich system which will plug into the Digitrax Loconet system allowing additional throttles to be plugged into it. It will work with infrared and radio throttles too.

layout without the worry of compatibility. Look for the DCC compatible or DCC conformant symbols in literature and on the box.

There are no standards governing the controller side of digital systems including throttle bus, plugs, ports and throttles themselves. Manufacturers have a free hand in the design of throttles and that is why the throttle and throttle bus protocol are important features to look at when making a decision. Some companies have shared throttle bus protocols to ensure compatibility with other systems. The Xpress-Net system

(X-bus) central to the Lenz system has been adopted by several manufacturers making the controllers cross-compatible in most cases. For example, a Roco 'Multimaus' controller will work with the Lenz system. Another example is the Z21 system which has throttle bus ports that supports X-bus and Digitrax Loconet controllers together with smartphone and tablet technology via a router making it a universal system.

Points to consider

Before dashing out to the model shop, think about the controllers and how

the system will support them. The following should help you write down a needs list so you do not buy a system which will be insufficient for your needs, or one with controllers incompatible with those used by your friends. NMRA DCC compatibility is desirable too as is avoiding spending more money than you need to by buying a system with too many features.

1 How many trains will be operated together at any one time on the layout? This will determine the required power output and number of controllers (throttles or cabs) needed for full operation. When calculating the power requirement, bear in mind that stationary locomotives draw power, especially if on-board sound or lights are active. Allow up to 0.5amps for each running train and 0.2amps for stationary locomotives with lights and sound active. Remember that rolling stock equipped with lighting will draw a small amount of current too - allow about 0.1amps. Add up the total and you will have a total current draw figure. Normally, a 5amp system will be adequate for a 'OO' gauge layout.

2 How many operators will be hosted on the layout at any one time? This will determine how

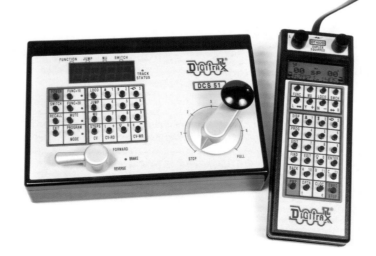

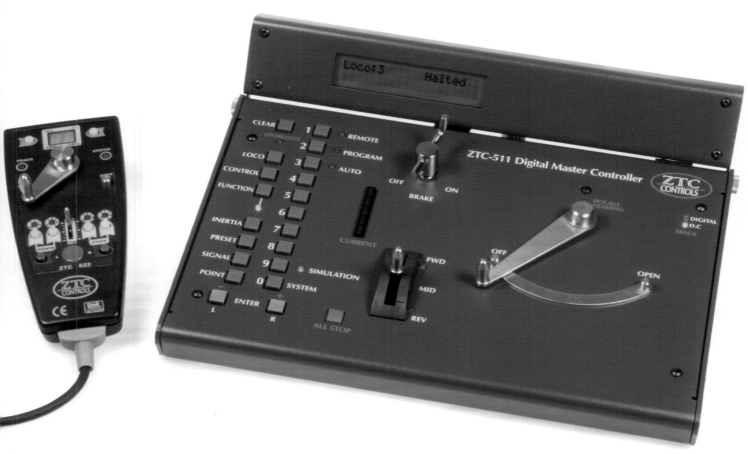

The Hornby Elite is a more advanced system than the Select, but is still based on a console with the controllers incorporated in the same box as the command station and booster. The Elite is however compatible with Hornby's RailMaster software and has recently been superseded by the Hornby eLink controller.

many throttles that you need for an operating session and the minimum number the system will support is something to consider.

3 Check the size of the controller or throttle. Can you read the throttle screen? Is it clear and large enough for your needs? Are the buttons clearly labelled and large enough for intuitive use when driving?

4 How many controller or throttle functions are needed? Given that digital sound locomotives are routinely available off-the-shelf, you may find that they require a large number of function controls to operate all of the on-board sounds. Choose a system with at least 20 function controls if planning to use digital sound locomotives.

5 Do you prefer a rotary knob or buttons to control the speed of a locomotive? Some throttles offer both knob and buttons whilst others work on buttons alone. The Digitrax DT400 series throttles have knob and button control for speed whilst Lenz offers two throttles, one with a control knob (LH90) and one with buttons (LH100). The Gaugemaster Prodigy throttle has a large user friendly control knob.

Above: ZTC offers a very smart master controller which is a console design. Its design is considerably different in that they attempt to replicate steam locomotive controls, something which might appeal to many modellers. ZTC has recently upgraded its master controller (ZTC-611) and owners of the ZTC-511 can take advantage of an upgrade service. The master controller also supports handheld throttles (ZTC-622).

Middle left: One of the simplest digital systems available is the Bachmann E-Z Command DCC system. A command station, booster and controller in one box, it delivers one amp of power and can handle up to nine locomotives. For many branch line and compact layouts, that might be the perfect system. An additional controller can be added to it, the Companion.

The ultimate destination for the instructions generated by the controller or throttle is the locomotive decoder. The instructions are interpreted by the command station, turned into digital packets which the decoder will understand and sent to the decoder via the power bus and track.

Right: Lenz offers two types of handheld throttle with its LZV100 base station. The LH90 has a control knob whilst the LH100 relies on buttons for speed step control. Both rely on menus to access many functions including programming and turnout control.

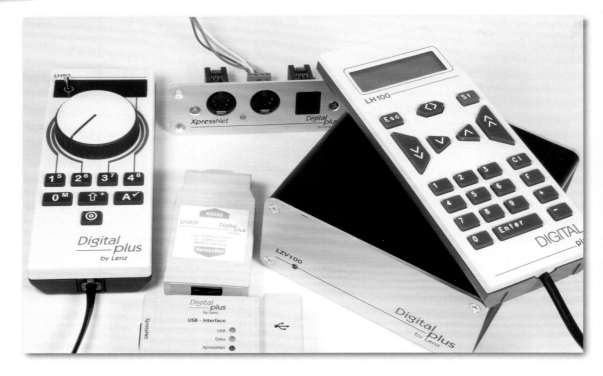

6 How many menus are incorporated in the throttle design? Some have a large number of buttons which provide almost all functions at one level, certainly no more than two. Others have fewer buttons but a larger screen enabling more functionality to be incorporated and accessed through menus rather than buttons.

7 How is the layout to be operated? Do you prefer to follow the train around the room or stay in one place at a fixed control panel? Some modellers are happy to sit at one place and watch trains run past. This type of operation suits the Hornby Elite or ZTC systems which are console type controllers. If, like me, you enjoy following the train around a large layout, consider handheld throttles and wireless control.

8 Will you use all of the features of a given system? If not, consider a lower cost system with fewer features and spend the remaining cash on additional decoders. A small branch line layout could easily be operated well with the entry level Bachmann

9005

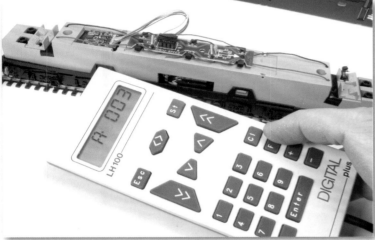

BENEFITS OF USING DCC

- DCC offers a realistic train driving experience with controllers that provide realistic driving controls.
- Control sound and lights independently as if you were in the cab of a real locomotive.
- Drive trains independently of other operators on the layout.
- Park where you want, drive where you want without the need for isolation switches.
- Double-heading, multiple working, twin power car operations and 'consisting' are simple to do.
- Enhance the driving experience with digital locomotive sound.
- No need to remember to switch in electrical sections or blocks.
- Greater flexibility of control with all of the layout being powered.
- Follow lineside signals (which can be digitally controlled with advanced systems).
- Peripheral devices make operation smoother on track formations such as reverse loops.
- Extra power can be incorporated when needed by adding boosters to the layout.
- Original investment is protected in most cases as individual systems are easily expanded and entry-level equipment can be incorporated when a more advanced system is purchased.
- The benefits of DCC can be realised on both large and small layouts, both steam and diesel outline.
- You drive the train as if it has its own power, rather than merely controlling the current in the track.
- Computer control can be added to some systems where a USB port is provided offering increased operational potential.

E-Z Command system with its nine locomotive address capacity.

9 Look at the throttle bus network and its features. Does your preferred system support one? Are fascia panels available so you can plug in handheld throttles around the layout? What additional features does the throttle bus support and will you find a use for them? Such features may include radio control and infrared.

10 The digital system used by your friends may have a bearing on your choice of system if you wish to use your own throttles to operate a friend's layout. Model railway club members may have to make a similar decision depending on the system used on club layouts. Give consideration to a universal throttle which can be operated with any digital systems throttle bus. For example, a smartphone can be used as a wireless throttle if the layout is equipped with the correct receiver and the appropriate app is loaded on the phone.

Console controllers

Console controllers are all-in-one systems with the command station, power station (booster) and throttle contained in one box. They are usually large and are designed for operations in the conventional sense in that the controls remain fixed in one location. Such systems include the Hornby Elite, Bachmann E-Z Command system, ZTC system and Digitrax Zephyr. Some allow for expansion by adding a throttle bus which enables the use of handheld throttles and roaming control.

Handheld controllers

The most common controller supplied with most DCC systems is the handheld throttle. They are fitted with a lead so they can be plugged into strategically positioned connection panels, also called throttle ports or fascia panels. The command station and power station (booster) will be contained in a separate box called a base station, probably located in an inconspicuous corner of the layout. Connection from the fascia

USEFUL RESOURCES

- www.digitrains.co.uk
- www.tonystrains.com
- www.digitrax.com
- www.dccconcepts.com
- www.dccsupplies.com
- www.lenz.com
- www.scc4dcc.co.uk
- www.dccspecialities.com
- www.ztccontrols.co.uk
- www.ncedcc.com
- www.bachmann.co.uk
- www.hornby.com

Above: A key part of using handheld throttles is the fascia plate or connection panels. They should be located at strategic places around the layout and are connected to the command or base station with a network of cables called the throttle or controller bus. It is usually very easy to set up. This is the Digitrax system.

Below: Bachmann Dynamis offers a completely different approach to DCC controllers, using a joystick for speed control and a menu system to access all of the features of the system. Features include the battery compartments (A); alpha-numeric keypad for number and word input (B); simple button control for running lights (C); a button to switch between turnout and locomotive control (D); menu button (E) and on-off switch (F). A joystick (G) is used for speed step control and menu navigation whilst direction change is through a simple button (H).

panels to the base station is via the throttle or controller bus.

Wireless controllers

Wireless controllers and throttles allow the modeller the freedom to follow a train around the layout without being tethered to a fascia panel, obeying signals and enjoying the experience of train driving exactly where the action is taking place. Congestion around fascia panels is avoided and operations can be enjoyed from any point in the layout room. In short, wireless operation is the ultimate in flexibility of train control and can increase the enjoyment of layout operation considerably.

A good example of an infrared system is the Bachmann Dynamis system which uses a line of sight infrared throttle to communicate with the command station. Receivers are placed around the layout and plugged directly into the DCC system itself. Conventional Digitrax throttles also include an infrared capability in addition to a cable as a standard feature. The correct infrared receiver has to be installed in the layout to take advantage of this feature.

Radio systems have grown in popularity and good examples include the MRC and Gaugemaster Prodigy together with the Digitrax Duplex Radio system. The Prodigy system uses

a receiver attachment which plugs into the back of the standard system whilst the Digitrax version works with a radio receiver fascia panel. One thing that all radio and infrared throttles need is an independent power supply. Batteries are the preferred choice and a good supply of rechargeable batteries should be to hand for operating sessions.

That question...

So, getting back to the original question about the digital system I would be most likely to recommend - the answer is that I can't provide a one size fits all answer! Perhaps the best advice I can offer is to try before you buy! Visit some digital

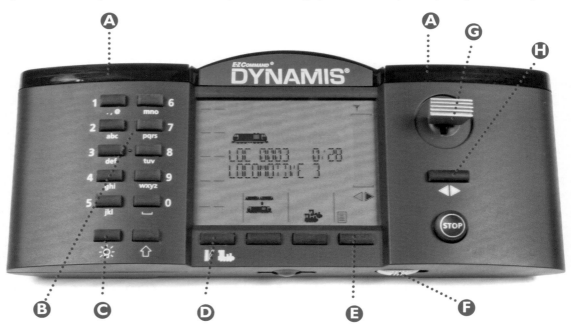

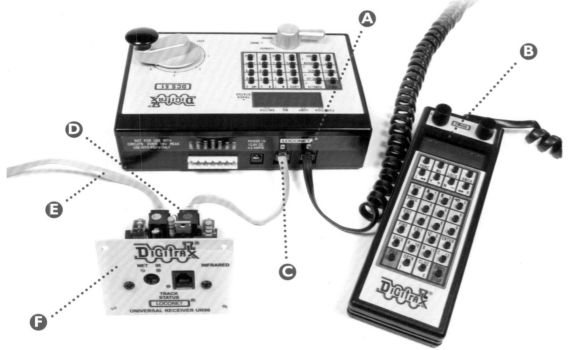

Above: **Key to using hand held throttles around the layout is the controller or throttle bus. This is a network of cables separate from the track power bus that connects any connection port or fascia panel to the digital system's base station. The throttle bus protocols are not governed by any DCC standards and may differ widely from manufacturer to manufacturer.**

Left: **A simplified throttle bus is demonstrated in this photograph. All hand held throttles (B) can be plugged directly into the back of a base station which has throttle bus ports (A). Throttle bus cables made up of readily available flat cable and RJ connectors (C) are plugged into the same ports and connect the fascia panels (F) together using ports in the rear (D). Each panel is connected to the next by 'daisy chaining with the flat cable (E).**

layouts, your local model railway club is a great place to start, to gain operating experience or ask exhibition layout operators if they would demonstrate their system to you so you can make an informed choice based on practical experience.

A fine example arose when buying an advanced DCC system for my home-based layout. Two American systems, both of which had excellent track records, made up the shortlist. One was the NCE system which is very simple to use yet feature rich. The other was Digitrax, more complex to use in

some respects but it comes with the highly functional Loconet throttle bus network.

There was very little to choose between them – they offered everything I needed for advanced layout control: both complied with DCC protocols as laid down by the NMRA and both companies offered excellent technical support. I opted for the latter simply due to the way in which the Digitrax DT400-series throttles fitted in my hand. I found the NCE throttles a tad too large for comfortable use over a prolonged operating session. The choice

between two systems was as simple as that.

When looking at digital command control for your new layout or when planning to convert an existing project, it's not always about the numbers. Test as many systems as you can to see which controller or throttle suits you the best. Be sure that it is a comfortable fit in terms of the number of functions and how it feels in your hand. Then you can enjoy an enhanced driving experience of your model trains which analogue control cannot possibly offer.

BULK
freight

You might imagine that the carriage of bulk freight flows in dedicated trainloads is a recent phenomenon but in fact the practice became widespread more than 50 years ago, as **Evan Green-Hughes** describes.

The transport of freight on the railways developed in a haphazard manner. The earliest lines were built to carry commodities such as coal short distances from the mine to rivers, harbours or canals. Within a short time railways connected many of the towns and cities of Great Britain and traders and manufacturers began to use them to distribute their products over wider areas than had been possible before.

In the second half of the 19th century the railways held almost universal power over the movement of freight within the country. Worried by this successive governments set about drafting legislation which required the railway companies to conduct their business in accordance with a number of set rules.

One of the most prominent of these set out a Common Carrier policy which required the railways to take any form of traffic offered and to move it at a price set by the government.

The idea behind this was to prevent companies taking on the best and most profitable traffic and turning down goods which were difficult to handle or uneconomic.

From that point on anyone could turn up at a station or a goods yard with a consignment, however small, and demand that the railway take it to any other station. This method of working involved railway staff locating suitable wagons, loading them and then arranging for them to be taken to the destination, a journey which might involve several separate trips, in between which a wagon might be shunted several times. Worse still, many consignments were so small that they would have to be grouped together with other deliveries in a van or truck and sorted by hand at each junction or shunting point.

This arrangement was still in force

in the early 1950s and British Railways offered a formidable service which covered every town and village in the country. It was, however, extremely costly to operate and contributed hugely to the railway's losses. In addition, competition from road transport was increasing and this, in an echo of the way that legislation has favoured road transport almost since the start, was never fettered by restrictive policies. As might be expected the road operators cherry picked the better work and left the rest to the railways.

Block trains

One way that the railways could counter this competition was to offer an improved service, particularly in the field of bulk goods, where a lot of the same commodity was to be moved from one place to another. Coal and other minerals, including limestone, were obvious traffics which had run in block trains but soon a surprising range of other products were too.

Stone was a prominent traffic flow from the West Country quarries and those in the Peak District as well as other areas. Highlights must include the distinctive bogie hoppers built by ICI for the movement of limestone from the Peak quarries. These vacuum brake bogie hoppers were built in the 1930s and continued in service into the 1990s seeing a wide variety of locomotives at the head of trains including Stanier '8F' 2-8-0s, BR '9F' 2-10-0s, Class 25s and in their final years Class 37s in pairs.

Perhaps the most obvious traffic flow to benefit from this type of train movement was coal, at that time virtually the only fuel used in power stations and for which there was still considerable domestic demand. Traditionally this had been moved in small four-wheel wagons little changed from those which had populated the earliest railways. Every day convoys of these wagons, marshalled in trains without continuous vacuum brakes, plodded up and down the trunk lines of the UK. Speeds were slow and costs were high because many of these trains were still unloaded by hand.

BR '9F' 2-10-0 92233, banked by a BR '4MT' 2-6-4T, blackens the sky as it crosses the virtually empty A74 main road with a Shap Quarry to Glasgow limestone train in 1965. W.J. Verden Anderson/Rail Archive Stephenson.

The first attempts to modernise this traffic came when some regions began to replace the ubiquitous 16ton four-wheeler with the 21ton hopper wagon. Fitted and unfitted versions of this truck were made and both offered the facility for rapid loading through their large uncovered top area and unloading through two sets of doors underneath. The fitted wagons were used on longer freight flows and could often be seen in rakes of 30-40 wagons moving between major cities, often hauled by large steam locomotives, such as the LNER's Robinson 'O4s', the LMS '8Fs' or the GWR's '28XX' 2-8-0s. Major efficiencies were achieved by using these larger wagons.

A modern approach

However there was much more work to be done and in 1964 British Railways commissioned two prototype wagons which transformed coal traffic and became a familiar sight for over 40 years. These new four-wheel wagons, later to be coded HAA, were built on a long wheelbase air-braked chassis capable of travelling at 45mph and could carry 32tons per wagon. Designed to work in rakes of up to 35 wagons the HAA's really revolutionary feature was that it was designed to be loaded from an overhead hopper and unloaded

automatically from below.

Large circular lines were built at collieries and power stations so that trains could be loaded and unloaded on the move, leading to huge efficiencies. The first power station to have coal delivered in this way was Cockenzie in Scotland in 1965 where it was estimated that 80 of the new wagons replaced around 1,500 conventional short-wheelbase four wheelers! These trains, which became known as 'Merry Go Rounds' for obvious reasons were

manual handling of the load at each end of the journey considerable savings could be made if the load was put into a box which could be removed with the load intact and delivered as one piece to the customer's premises.

Containers were already a common sight on UK railways and a set of standard specifications was produced by the Railway Clearing House in the 1930s. These allowed for a number of standard wooden containers, all designed to travel on four-wheel wagons. Prior to

"The first attempts to modernise coal traffic came when some regions began to replace 16ton mineral wagons with 20ton hoppers. Longer coal flows between major cities were often formed of 30-40 wagons hauled by large locomotives including 2-8-0s."

firmly part of the scene in the final years of the steam era, but were usually hauled by diesels due to the air brake being installed, with initially Brush Type 4s (Class 47s) being the normal motive power.

Another obvious target for those seeking to modernise the railway was container traffic. As one of the most significant costs in moving freight was the

the 1960s these were more commonly accommodated within normal goods workings as single wagons and the pace of delivery of goods was as pedestrian as it was for other forms as a result.

Trains of containers had been tried by a number of the pre-nationalisation railway companies, in particular by the LNER, which ran block container trains of meat from Scotland to London but these did

Former ROD 'O4' 2-8-0 63744 comes round the East Coast Main Line curve at Chaloners Whin with a down iron ore train in 1955. Kenneth Field/Rail Archive Stephenson.

not see widespread use. In the 1950s the concept was re-worked and in 1959 British Railways introduced its express 'Condor' (Containers Door to Door) service. This used 75-mph-rated four-wheel vacuum-fitted Conflat wagons and ran from London to Glasgow each night, the idea being that goods despatched before the close of business in the capital could be in Glasgow by the start of trade the following day.

Immortalised by Terence Cuneo in one of his famous paintings, the 'Condor' was usually hauled by a pair of the spectacularly unsuccessful Metro-Vick Co-Bo diesels, but due to the unreliability of these locomotives the train often saw other classes at the head, including steam.

Modern intermodal

In 1961 the London Midland Region introduced an updated container service between London and Manchester which used metal boxes, rather than wooden, and which had an enhanced method of loading and securing them to the wagons.

Unlike the standard containers used on the 'Condor' these units had to work between specially-equipped yards as they could only be unloaded by specially made lifts. These didn't last long as international standards for containers had come into force, giving rise to the familiar 'boxes which we see today. Initially some of these were carried on converted Lowmac wagons but the infamous Dr Beeching had proposed an expansion of container services and in 1964 he authorised the finance to enable British Railways to commence work on introducing a 'liner' service.

These were to convey the new standard containers on specially-built air-braked bogie wagons between prominently situated railheads and would become branded as 'Freightliner'. These were immediately successful and within five years there were 140 services a day serving 30 terminals. Early trains carried only British Railways' own Freightliner containers and thus presented a uniform appearance from end to end but in more modern times containers owned by others have come to be carried.

Again the versatile Class 47s were the preferred traction in the 1960s but other types of locomotive did appear from time to time.

Road transport onwards from the Freightliner terminals allowed the railways to compete with roads, leading

to a great deal of traffic, which might otherwise have been lost, remaining with the railways and the Freightliner name is still part of the railway scene today.

Car trains

However the roads were not always completely detrimental to the railways - a great deal of block traffic was built up to serve the expanding motor industry. At that time large quantities of parts were being sourced from outside the main car plants and, due to the inadequate state of the roads, the best way to have these delivered was by rail.

One of the biggest users of the railways was the Pressed Steel Company which had several plants, including those at Oxford and Swindon which were

producing pressings for the car industry. Many of these were delivered to sites such as Longbridge in Birmingham on 'company' trains of standard four-wheel box vans. This traffic increased massively in the immediate post-steam era when long-wheelbase vans conveyed huge quantities of parts. 1974 saw Swindon supplying Longbridge with body panels for 4,000 Austin Allegros every week by this method.

Completed cars were also moved by rail from the factories to the docks for export, with notable flows being from places such as Ford in Dagenham to Garston Docks in Liverpool. Many were carried on flat wagons similar to bogie bolsters, some of which had been converted from the chassis of redundant passenger coaches. Later double-deck

Top: Thompson 'B1' 4-6-0 61062 makes light work of a rake of empty bogie bolster wagons as it heads north on the East Coast Main Line near Beningbrough in summer 1960. Cecil Ord/Rail Archive Stephenson.

Above: BR '3MT' 2-6-2T 82016 comes through the loop at Marchwood with an empty oil tank train for Fawley on April 28 1962. Mike Fox/Rail Archive Stephenson.

transporters were used which offered some protection to the vehicles. Early car trains were often steam-hauled but once the double-deck transporters arrived the necessity for air braking meant that diesel or electric haulage was the norm.

A considerable source of traffic prior to the Channel Tunnel and more widespread use of air freight was that of fruit and perishables from mainland Europe to the UK. The bulk of this was carried in special long-wheelbase 45ton vans which were shipped across from Europe on the train ferry with their loads still in place. These vans were equipped

Heavy metal

Perhaps one of the most spectacular bulk trains to operate during the steam and early diesel period was the bulk iron-ore trains between Tyne Dock and Consett. Raw materials arrived by ship and were transferred into specially built bogie hoppers for transfer up the steep gradients to the Consett steelworks. In the latter days of steam these trains were worked by BR Standard '9Fs' modified with large air pumps so that they could work the discharge doors on the wagons but with an incline which was in places as steep as 1-in-40 most trains required a second such locomotive to

> "BR Standard '9Fs' were modified with large air pumps so that they could work the discharge doors on the Tyne Dock-Consett iron wagons."

with both air and vacuum brakes and had large sliding doors to each side, as well as special ventilation grilles designed to keep the load cool during transit.

Prior to 1962 most of these vans had originated in Europe but in that year British Railways commissioned two batches, later coded VJX, for this traffic. Long trains of these vans were commonplace in the South, where they were often steam hauled, particularly in the summer months when there were considerable imports of fresh fruit. This traffic eventually built up to the stage where a £2m terminal was opened at Paddock Wood, which could receive up to 75 wagons a day for rapid unloading.

bank at the back end. The performance of these locomotives was explosive and for those who saw or heard this spectacle it is a never to be forgotten memory. Prior to the '9Fs' there were 'Q7' 0-8-0s to enjoy and even in the diesel era pairs of Class 24s proved a stirring sight.

Other bulk iron-ore flows were worked to steelworks in South Wales and Scotland, amongst others, but none were quite as spectacular as the Consett operation.

Bulk trains were also worked containing other raw materials, for instance soda ash for the glassmaking industry. One of the flows which was

vastly improved in the British Railways era was that between Wallerscote on Merseyside and Larbert in Scotland. This material had traditionally been packed in 2cwt bags and conveyed in standard vans, a process that was made worse by the requirement to tranship the load onto road transport for the final part of its journey in Scotland.

In 1966 a fleet of new hopper wagons was purchased which allowed for automatic loading on Merseyside, as well as transfer to specially-built road vehicles in Scotland and automated discharge at the final destination. Interestingly this flow, which was of two trains a week of 25 wagons each, was one of the first examples of a partnership between British Railways and the private sector, as it was jointly financed by United Glass, a Scottish road transport operator and BR itself.

Stanier 'Black Five' 44677, with a coal weighing tender, climbs through Glen Ogle with a cement train on the Oban line in 1958 formed entirely of Presflo cement wagons. W.J.Verden Anderson/ Rail Archive Stephenson.

**Above: In 1957 Fowler
'4F' 0-6-0 44086 passes
Grange-over-Sands with
an empty coke train from
Barrow-in-Furness to the
North East.**
Gordon Hepburn/Rail
Archive Stephenson.

**Left: Class 25 D5275
passes Chinley with a
Tunstead to Northwich
ICI lime stone train on
May 21 1966 formed of
ICI bogie hoppers.**
Brian Stephenson.

Bulk variety

Another commodity that made the transition from 2cwt bags to special rail wagons was cement, which was then accommodated in 'Presflo' wagons of the type made immortal by Hornby Dublo and Airfix in model form. These allowed for loading and discharge using compressed air and were painted in the liveries of the companies whose products they were carrying. Block trains of these were a common sight in the early 1960s when many of the country's major construction projects were in progress. Later larger four-wheel wagons were produced which were more in the style of tankers, though they had depressed centres to aid the unloading process.

Wagons similar in style to the bulk hoppers were used for the carriage of grain from various ports of import to Scotland for use in the whisky trade. Many of these were introduced in the mid 1960s and were another example of private investment in the state railway, with one single order in 1966 being for 115 wagons. Although these ran in bulk trains they were not necessarily all for one manufacturer with the result that a colourful train of wagons in the liveries of different private owners often ran, something which can be a boon for modellers seeking to introduce something different to a layout set in state-owned times.

Another raw material which travelled extensively by rail in steam days was china clay, once extensively quarried in Cornwall. This was used in many industrial processes, including papermaking and production of tableware. For many years the simple four-wheel wagon with its distinctive tarpaulin cover, and later the signature tent-like blue roof, was the staple wagon for this trade and bulk trains were despatched to many parts of the country, as well as individual wagons to smaller locations. Later these vacuum-braked wagons were replaced by modified HAA wagons which had had a roof cover fitted

BR 'Britannia' 4-6-2 70011 climbs Grayrigg bank near Lambrigg with a train load of ballast on April 14 1967.
D Hepburne Scott/Rail Archive Stephenson.

and later still by large bogie wagons of around 100tons capacity.

Liquid gold

In the years immediately before and after Nationalisation one of the biggest growth areas for bulk traffic was the carriage of oil and its refined products such as petrol, diesel and aviation fuel. Refineries such as Fawley, near Southampton, were established in the 1920s but were massively expanded in the 1940s and 1950s as demands for their products expanded.

Fawley sent out daily trains of four-wheel tank wagons to destinations all over the South of England, many to bulk

storage facilities such as that at Hamble, which was only just on the other side of Southampton Water. The site also received incoming crude oil traffic from sites such as Wytch Farm, a commercial well in nearby Dorset.

For much of the post-war period block trains were also worked from refineries to local distribution depots from where the fuel was picked up by road tanker for delivery to garages and other consumers. Improvements in the 1960s saw the 12ft wheelbase tankers replaced by more suitable 15ft wheelbase 45tonners and again an outbreak of private owner liveries. Steam traction was extensively used on oil trains, although there were always a couple of empty wagons marshalled at the front and back of the train to provide a sort of barrier and reduce the amount of hot sparks falling on the loaded tank wagons.

Most of this bulk traffic has been lost today to fixed pipelines and even the local distribution depots have all closed down as it has proved more economic for operators to send articulated road tankers direct to the refinery to pick up loads. Similar tank wagons were used in the 1950s and 1960s for a host of other products, many of which were worked in block trains, and these included bitumen, caustic soda and acid.

Less well-known bulk trains conveyed foodstuffs such as meat and fish from Scotland to the South or milk from the West of England to London and other large cities. Many of these ran at night so were not commonly seen but are interesting because they conveyed perishables and were therefore worked at express speeds. Fish and meat travelled in specially made insulated vans,

some of which were painted white, and often were hauled by Class 1 engines such as Gresley 'Pacifics', though more commonly by mixed traffic designs such as the 'V2' 2-6-2s.

Also worked at express speeds were the overnight trains which conveyed newspapers from London, Edinburgh and Manchester to towns and cities all over the country. Within these trains were facilities to sort newspapers into bundles and some of the coaches were provided with longitudinal tables running the length of the vehicle on which this work could be carried out. Stock was usually full-length parcels vehicles, full brakes or specially-converted vehicles although it was not unknown for non-corridor CCTs and other such vehicles to be used.

As can be seen there were many bulk freight flows involving the use of one-product trains in the transition era. Careful selection of a subject can produce a colourful and unusual collection of vehicles, while older types can legitimately be included as well. Bulk freight flows are by no means a preserve of the modern railway scene and, correctly modelled, can provide a point of interest on any layout.

Top: BR '9F' 2-10-0 92064 coasts towards South Pelaw Junction with a Consett to Tyne Dock train of iron ore empties on August 29 1965. Brian Stephenson.

Above: Representing the new form of freight movement for the 1960s, Class 47 D1951 has just passed Shap Quarry with an up Freightliner train in late 1967. Gordon Hepburn/ Rail Archive Stephenson.

Building
A SIGNAL GANTRY

Signals make all the difference to a model railway.
Mike Wild explains how a Ratio Pratt Truss gantry was
modified and extended to span a five-track main line.

The Ratio kits range of signals and components is an excellent source of materials for enhancing and detailing railway scenes. Signals are essential, but in some locations the large number of arms required means installing a gantry.

For Twelve Trees Junction we've assembled three gantries to support signals across the station throat and also across the five track main line on the approach to the station.

The two gantries at the station are built as per the instructions supplied by Ratio, except for shortening one of the legs on one gantry to accommodate positioning on the platform. However, the third gantry across the main lines

needed altogether different treatment.

To span the full five tracks we used two Pratt Truss gantry kits and modified them to span the full width of the running lines. A secondary modification was to shorten the overhang on one end of the gantry so that it didn't foul on the carriage shed building.

Painting a fine structure like these gantries can be a time consuming process, but if you have access to an airbrush life can be made much simpler. Using an airbrush means that fine painting can be achieved around all the angles of the gantry frame for a quality result. The alternative is brush painting which, while needing more time, will also result in a good finish with care.

The main paint colour used on our

models is Lifecolor's BR freight grey with BR bauxite brush painted onto the upper timber platform and Lifecolor burned black for details such as the smoke deflectors and ladders.

The final additions to this gantry are signal arms. These are from Ratio's 476 kit which contains a selection of round post signals and posts which are suitable for use with the gantry. These are assembled separately then fitted onto the gantry.

With the gantry completed it adds a significant scenic feature to the London end of Twelve Trees Junction while the two smaller gantries around the station offer much needed detail at the platform ends.

The completed five track span signal gantry really looks the part across the main lines on Twelve Trees Junction. A Maunsell 'King Arthur' 4-6-0 passes underneath with an express.

Product	Manufacturer	Cat No.
Pratt Truss gantry	Ratio	478
Round post signals	Ratio	476

WHAT WE USED

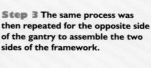

Step 3 The same process was then repeated for the opposite side of the gantry to assemble the two sides of the framework.

Step 4 Because we shortened the far end of the gantry overhang we used spare triangular braces at the top of the supporting bars as well as the bottom for a neat finish.

Step 1 As this project involves modifications to the original kit design, the first step was to cut the bases and supporting legs from the fret and assemble them. This gave us the outer markers allowing a measurement to be taken for the width of the gantry.

Step 2 Having worked out the width of the gantry at 290mm we marked the distance between the two supports on a scrap of wood as a guide. Using two gantry kits we trimmed the inner ends of two main supports and joined them together to create one side of the gantry.

Step 5 Next the upper walkway was added using three full sections and one cut down to suit the length of the gantry.

Step 6 The ladders supplied with the kit need to be cut carefully from the sprue as the plastic mouldings are very fine. These were fitted and their supports added.

Step 7 Five smoke deflectors were added underneath the gantry frame. As only two come in each kit, the centre deflector was cut from 1mm thick plasticard and its edges shaped to match those in the kit.

Step 8 Having completed construction the gantry then needed to be painted. Lifecolor BR freight grey was used for the main structure with the same manufacturer's BR bauxite for the walkway. The ladders are painted with white for the bottom four rungs and Lifecolor burned black for the remaining steps.

Step 9 Next a selection of signal arms were painted to suit the gantry. It controls a complex junction, so a large number of posts and arms were required.

Step 10 Having fitted a set of posts and arms onto the walkway the gantry is now ready to be fitted to the layout. The gantry was fixed in place with contact adhesive.

Urban SKYLINE

I f you have ever travelled into or out of London on the Southern Region then you'll know what we are aiming for. Those rows of towering buildings which dominate the skyline are an important part of this model, but with space at a premium we turned to one of the most useful building types available – the low relief structure.

Low relief buildings are essentially thin fascias which offer a frontage but without any great depth. There are numerous ready made resin low relief buildings, but for Twelve Trees Junction we wanted to create a more unique feel. We turned to the Skytrex range of castings and scratchbuilding to create the backdrop.

There is a collection of buildings along the backscene, all of which help create that skyline image. These consist of a bus garage tucked down below railway

With the backdrop complete a Bulleid 'Q1' leads a long van train onto the slow lines as a 4-SUB EMU departs from the station.

The skyline is an essential part of Twelve Trees Junction to give it that London suburb feel. **Phil Parker** and **Mike Wild** explain how the backdrop was created using low relief buildings.

level behind the carriage shed, a pair of four storey 1960s flats, four tenement buildings and a low relief factory and boiler house. The factory and boiler house are the only scratchbuilt buildings, although the blocks of flats have been extended with a basement section.

Planning process

One of the areas which we felt had let *Hornby Magazine*'s previous layouts down was a lack of backscene detail. Artistic painting skills aren't strong in the team when it comes to backscenes, so at best backdrops have represented distant hills

and at worst feature plain blue painted backboards.

With Twelve Trees Junction's urban setting a plain blue backboard behind the roadway just wouldn't have looked right, but rather than go for the simple option of using a printed backscene we decided to invest time selecting and building a collection of low relief structures, both residential and industrial.

Each one was positioned roughly on the layout first to gauge how they would look which resulted in some modifications to the original planned layout for the structures. Once satisfied and with the roadway in place the next

WHAT WE USED

Product	Manufacturer	Cat No.	Quantity
1960s flats single storey front panel	Skytrex	4/033	8
1960s flats roof unit with parapet	Skytrex	4/036	2
Tenement building rear walls	Skytrex	4/021	4
Right facing Northlight building façade	Skytrex	4/002	3

task was to clean up the resin castings from Skytrex and add colour to them so that they could be fixed in place.

The most complicated section of the backdrop was along the road where it dropped away from its maximum to minimum height. We wanted the four tenement buildings to step down to road level and to achieve this a wooden plinth was made from two pieces of identically shaped 6mm MDF which stepped down above the road level. Wills brick sheeting was added to the front of this to complete the look of the area.

Similarly the basement of one of the two four storey flats is also sunk below road level at one end as the road levels out at the bottom of the hill.

Painting the bricks

When you look at a wall closely few of the bricks are the same colour, and there is a huge range of tones. This is why builders will mix the bricks from several deliveries. Failing to do this can result in a wall with stripes of similar colours. This is even with the benefit of modern mixing and firing methods to produce consistent results. Older bricks that have been subject to years of weather and dirt from the atmosphere show even

more variety.

From a distance though, brick walls look brown in most areas. The actual shade can vary depending on the part of the country and in London, will be a yellow or even cream colour. This is the way we see a model wall. Because of this, there isn't any real need to colour each brick face individually – if you get the overall effect people will simply see the model as being 'right'.

There are lots of ways to colour a model wall. The biggest problem is that there is brick colour and mortar colour and they mustn't mix. Painting the surfaces almost always results in some colour seeping into the mortar lines which then needs to be repainted and this is how we painted the retaining walls along the layout – mortar was added using thinned enamel followed by dry brushing of the grey engineer's brick colour (see Scenery feature on pages 86-93). Working with a small piece of sponge rather than a brush is sometimes more effective for this method, but it's still fiddly.

A far cleaner method is to paint the mortar and then rub the brick surface with pencil crayons. The colour should be picked up on the brick faces and only

the faces.

Some experimentation with the actual pencil crayons is a good idea. The material you made the wall from will affect how rough it is and how hard a pencil will work best. I've collected quite a lot of shades of brown from both stationers and art shops. Work on a small area first to find the best pencil and then carry on over the rest of the building.

The method is simple – colour the walls with a mid-brown shade and then work over them again with other colours. This produces a variety of subtle tones that should look about right. Best of all, it's simple, clean work ideal for whiling away time in front of the television - the sort of job you can do in the warm during Winter.

Once the brickwork is finished, it probably needs a bit of dirt and here weathering powders come to the fore. You may find giving the brickwork a light spray of matt varnish is helpful in giving the powder something to adhere to, but again, this will vary from model to model.

The results of planning the backdrop and the methods for creating the brick colours speak for themselves and give

USEFUL LINKS

Skytrex
www.skytrexmodel
railways.com

Step 1 The aim of the backdrop is to create a London style skyline. The main components are Skytrex resin castings for tenement buildings, 1960s flats and Northlight factory buildings.

Step 2 Having mocked up the parts for the flats we decided they needed to be raised higher for a better effect. Brick embossed plasticard was the medium of choice to extend the buildings and add a basement.

Step 3 The bus depot at the end of the layout is set below the level of the carriage sheds, but adds a welcome change in height. Again Skytrex resin castings are the source of components for this.

Step 4 Bricks show plenty of shades with a mix of browns, and some of them even quite orange. You can see the variation in tones created by age and weathering on the older buildings whereas the new one on the right is almost a single colour. The darkest bricks are purple engineering bricks added for decoration.

Step 5 This is our collection of coloured pencil crayons. These are bought from art shops and vary in hardness. Normally the harder types work best but some surfaces require a softer lead to get the colour to stick.

Step 6 The bus depot is a resin building. Colouring starts with a coat of Humbrol 121 to represent mortar. Starting with a Derwent Artists Burnt Sienna pencil, the main blocks of colour are filled in. At this stage it looks terrible but working over the areas with different shades builds up a depth of colour.

Step 7 Getting colour in to the nooks and crannies often requires the pencil tip to be shaped. Rubbing the lead on a coarse file produces a flat and wide tip that will get into awkward corners such as around the drainpipes on the tenement building.

Step 8 On a reasonably new building, a couple of similar colours worked over the surface will be enough for the job. The flats are supposed to be recent additions to the Twelve Trees skyline so they are still very clean. The window frames are painted with Humbrol 147 and then infilled with satin black. From normal viewing distances, the lack of high gloss glass looks very realistic.

Step 9 Older buildings benefit from weathering. While the brick colours provide a good starting point, working the surface over with weathering powders finishes the job off. The green colour is rising damp and will be toned down once the brown is added. Extra dirt collects in the very corners where it can be difficult to get the pencil colour to take so it's worth doing this on any building.

Step 10 With the tenement buildings fully painted and weathered a supporting plinth cut from MDF was made to step them down above road level. It has been covered with Wills brick sheets which still required painting at this point.

Step 11 To finish the tenement buildings grey coloured paper was added behind the openings to give them more depth. All the buildings are fixed to the backscene boards with contact adhesive.

Step 12 The bus depot backdrop sits behind the carriage shed and provides more welcome skyline detail.

Building BRIDGES

Railway lines would sometimes call for complex bridges to be built to carry roads or other railways across at awkward angles. **Phil Parker** explains how a bow-topped plate girder bridge was built as a major scenic aspect of Twelve Trees Junction.

A BR '4MT' 2-6-0 leads an engineers' working through the newly installed bridge. The bow-topped structure makes for a defining feature on Twelve Trees Junction.

Right: Viewed from above a pair of Class 33s pass through the bridge. Further low relief buildings will be added to the right of the bridge to complete the backdrop.

Twelve Trees Junction presented one of the most interesting bridge projects that we have undertaken. Following installation of the double junction and the subsequent track alignment it meant providing some means to carry a road over the top of the railway.

Not every structure on a layout can be picked out of a plans book and this is a prime example. Initial thoughts turned to commercially available structures. However, such is the angle of the railway that this just wasn't physically possible in the 3ft baseboard width of the layout.

The solution was to custom build a bridge to fit the site. After looking through books for inspiration we hit upon the idea of a double-span bow-topped plate girder bridge. The spans would be skewed to take into account the steep angle of the track to be bridged.

With time tight, construction needed to be as simple as possible. Bridge sides fitted to a roadway seemed the simplest solution, and all I had to do was produce them. Fortunately we had some long

sheets of plasticard to hand as each part would be longer than standard A4 sized pieces. Our stocks came from a model boat supplier but large sheets are often available cheaply from suppliers at model railway exhibitions. You have to collect though as posting A1 size plastic sheet isn't possible.

Building a model for a specific site is made a lot easier if you can try it in the space before progressing very far. Sometimes it even makes sense to mock the model up in cardboard before cutting the final materials. Here, we started with an overlong roadway made from 3mm thick plywood and Blu-tacked the plastic sides to it, gambling that they wouldn't need much alteration.

The first attempt showed that our original sketched out heights for the sides were too high and also that the sides were too long. Having taken stock, remeasured and decided on a new height for the sides we went back to the workbench to make the changes.

Marking out the sides proved to be the

biggest challenge of the entire project. The top edge of the bridge needed to be a smooth curve of about 2ft radius. Casting around, I couldn't find anything that was remotely this size. In the end we tried to bend a strip of wood between two points and draw along this. The results weren't bad but still had a flat apex.

The second attempt at marking out involved sticking a couple of 24 inch radius SMP point plans together, cutting along the curved rail and using this as a template. While still not perfect, it worked well enough to produce sides that could have the ribbing detail added. The corners were rounded off by cutting around a five pence coin.

At this point, someone pointed out what we should have done. In our track building toolbox are some Tracksetta strips. Each is a flat piece of aluminium cut to a curve, including a 24in diameter panel. We could have used this as a ruler and produced a nice neat curve. Better still, several radii are available so we could have had a choice!

STEP-BY-STEP | BUILDING A BOW-TOPPED PLATE GIRDER BRIDGE

Step 1 The location for the bridge was complicated by the angle of the track against the road on a higher level. Having tried commercial products, the only way forward was to scratchbuild a set of sides.

Step 2 The first attempt was no more than some roughly cut bridge sides made from 1mm thick Plasticard and fitted to the plywood roadway with Blu-Tack. At this stage we decided that the embankment sides were too close together and the bridge sides were both too long and too high, but at least the overall look was right.

Step 3 Tracksetta tools are curved metal strips that will slide between the rails of 'OO' track (also available in 'N' gauge) and the radius of each is marked on it. They are intended to help modellers lay smooth curves but also make excellent curved rulers and would have been ideal for marking out the top edges of the bridge sides.

Step 4 While the Tracksetta might be the best tool to mark out a 24inch radius curve, we used a couple of SMP point plans stuck to cardboard and then cut out along the curved rails. A CD marker pen run along the inside edge marked the Plasticard which was then cut by eye with an Olfa Plasticard cutter, which is slightly neater than a knife, although a craft knife would work perfectly well with care.

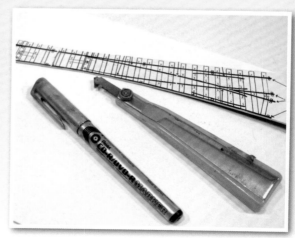

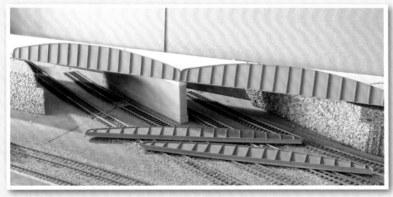

Step 5 A real bridge would be covered in thousands of rivets but for speed, we decided to limit the detailing to adding ribbing on the sides. A 6mm wide strip of 0.5mm thick plasticard runs along the top with the rest of the ribs being made of the same material. Because the bridge runs along the backscene, we didn't add ribs to the hidden sides. A support pillar is made from thick card covered in brick embossed plasticard.

Step 6 As the bridge crosses a baseboard joint, it has to be removable to transport. Screwing the ends into wooden blocks set into the embankment sides holds it in place and stops the flexible structure from twisting.

Step 7 Finally in position, the embankment sides are built up from Wills brick sheets. To give the bridge sides some colour, they have been sprayed with car primer from an aerosol – a good match for the grey that these structures were normally painted in.

Step 8 The final addition to the bridge is the road surface which has been cut from artists mounting board and topped with Wills York paving plastic components for the pavements. The entire bridge is removable with the screws being covered by road vehicles when on display.

WHAT WE USED

Product	Manufacturer	Cat No.
Scenecraft EMU carriage shed	www.bachmann.co.uk	44-083
Ratio carriage cleaning platforms	www.peco-uk.com	544
1mm thick plasticard	www.slatersplastikard.com	0130
2mm thick plasticard	www.slatersplastikard.com	0180
Grey primer	www.halfords.co.uk	451542

Carriage shed

Goods sheds, stations and locomotive depots are all regularly modelled, and although carriage sheds are lesser known they are equally enthralling subjects. **Mike Wild** explains how a carriage shed was installed and detailed for Twelve Trees Junction.

Filled with a selection of Southern Region EMUs including Hornby 2-BIL and 5-BEL units and a Bachmann 4-CEP, the completed carriage shed captures the look part of these substantial buildings.

The Southern Region's proliferation of Electric Multiple Units (EMUs) was vast and so was the need to provide suitable facilities for maintenance and storage of the ever expanding fleet in the 1950s and 1960s.

There was already a collection of established locations, but with new traction entering service more were needed. Amongst the locations chosen for this in the Kent Coast Electrification Scheme of the 1950s were Ashford, Stewarts Lane, Ramsgate, Chart Leacon and Hither Green. However, these locations also included sheds such as those at Grove Park near London which had an 820ft long, six road carriage shed.

One of the problems of recreating a carriage shed in model form is the sheer size of the buildings. Grove Park was designed to handle 12 coach formations, indoors, and would require a building just short of 11ft long in 'OO' gauge to model it in full scale.

Naturally any model of a carriage shed is likely to be a shortened version of a real location and that is what we set out to recreate on Twelve Trees Junction. Having previously modelled goods sheds, stations and locomotive depots in steam and diesel eras, we felt a carriage shed would present a new opportunity for the build and something different as the end result.

The main component of the carriage shed is Bachmann's Scenecraft carriage shed section (Cat No. 44-083). These have become difficult to find of late, but after an extensive search we located the four buildings we needed to create a structure capable of housing a four-car

EMU. Each section comes with shed road numbers and joining pieces to fill the gap between the main metal sheds. The end result is a good looking model and a distinctive building.

The interior fittings of carriage sheds varied. Some had raised walkways but others didn't while some featured full concrete floors with the track set in and others had concrete walkways between ballasted tracks. For this model we've used a combination of concrete walkways between ballasted tracks with two raised walkways. Because of the length of the shed we have only detailed the first 12in of the shed at each end as the centre section can't be seen from the outside.

The step by step guide explains how we went about installing and detailing the carriage shed for Twelve Trees Junction.

STEP-BY-STEP — BUILDING A CARRIAGE SHED IN 'OO' GAUGE

Step 1 First, the shed buildings need to be laid out. Fillets are supplied with each shed to fill in the gap between the main walls in two thicknesses. Select the right width and slot them into the walls using contact adhesive to fix them in place.

Step 2 With the carriage sheds laid out over the track – see feature on pages 20-27 – they will just accommodate four tracks, leaving space for Ratio walkways between each pair of tracks.

Step 3 To provide a concrete depot floor, strips of 2mm thick plasticard were cut to size to fit between the sleeper ends. The outer pieces have been cut to fit between the sleeper ends and the base of the shed building. Only short lengths have been used to give the illusion of the full interior.

Step 4 Ratio carriage cleaning walkways were then built up and positioned on top of the 'concrete' floors. These had to be extended to suit the length of the interior visible.

Step 6 Viewed from the outside, the compromised length of the walkways and floors is obvious without any units inside, but it will look the part once complete.

Step 5 With walkways and all of the floor sections in place temporarily, the shed interior is starting to take shape.

The four section carriage shed offers an impressive structure on Twelve Trees Junction.

Step 7 To add extra detail in front of the shed a barrow crossing was added using section of 1mm thick plasticard cut to size. Again these components were laid loose initially so that they could be painted away from the layout.

Step 8 With all the plastic cut to size the carriage shed is already looking much more realistic. The components were then numbered underneath so that we knew where each part went after painting.

Step 9 The final step before painting was to glue the walkways onto the 'concrete' floors. This was done using Deluxe Materials Plastic Magic liquid glue.

Step 11 As with the floors ballasting extends only partway into the shed which will suffice for most viewing angles. Woodland Scenics fine and medium grade grey blend ballast was mixed together then carefully sprinkled into place. Dilute PVA glue mixed with water to a 50:50 ratio holds it all in place.

Step 10 All of the plastic parts were then painted with grey car primer, left to dry, then glued in place on the layout with contact adhesive leaving just ballasting and third-rail installation, outside the shed, to complete the area.

Step 12 The finishing touches for Twelve Trees Junction's carriage shed are numbers above each track – 1 always being closest to the main running line. The number boards, supplied with the carriage sheds, were fixed to the building with superglue completing the external detailing process.

The *Hornby Magazine*
Gallery

Spotlighting the very best layouts and photography to feature in *Hornby Magazine*, this gallery will inspire and delight. Editor **Mike Wild** presents a small selection of 2013's best feature layouts.

New Mills

Capturing the majesty of Stanier's 'Princess Royal' class 'Pacifics', 46200 Princess Royal thunders along the West Coast Main Line on New Mills. This main line layout features non-stop action on four tracks – two on an upper level and two on a lower level. New Mills featured in HM69. Trevor Jones.

Selsdon Park

Steve Jones' Selsdon Park is usually populated with 1990s period rolling stock, but for a special feature in Hornby Magazine he backdated the model to the late 1950s and early 1960s. With a collection of London Transport RT and RM buses below a Maunsell 'Schools' 4-4-0 slows for the station. Selsdon Park featured in HM72. Mike Wild.

82G – Bristol, Templecombe Road Shed

Motive power depots are popular subjects for models with 82G – Bristol Templecombe Road Shed being one of the best examples. Modelled in 'O' gauge a GWR '2251' 0-6-0 simmers beneath the crane on the lifting road. 82G featured in **HM74.** Mike Wild.

Holcombe Brook and Tottington

An Ivatt '2MT' 2-6-0 eases its rake of 20ton hopper across Tottington viaduct. This viaduct is one of three individual scenes which make up Peter Crichton's layout which he purchased and converted to DCC control in 2012. Holcombe Brook and Tottington featured in HM65. Mike Wild.

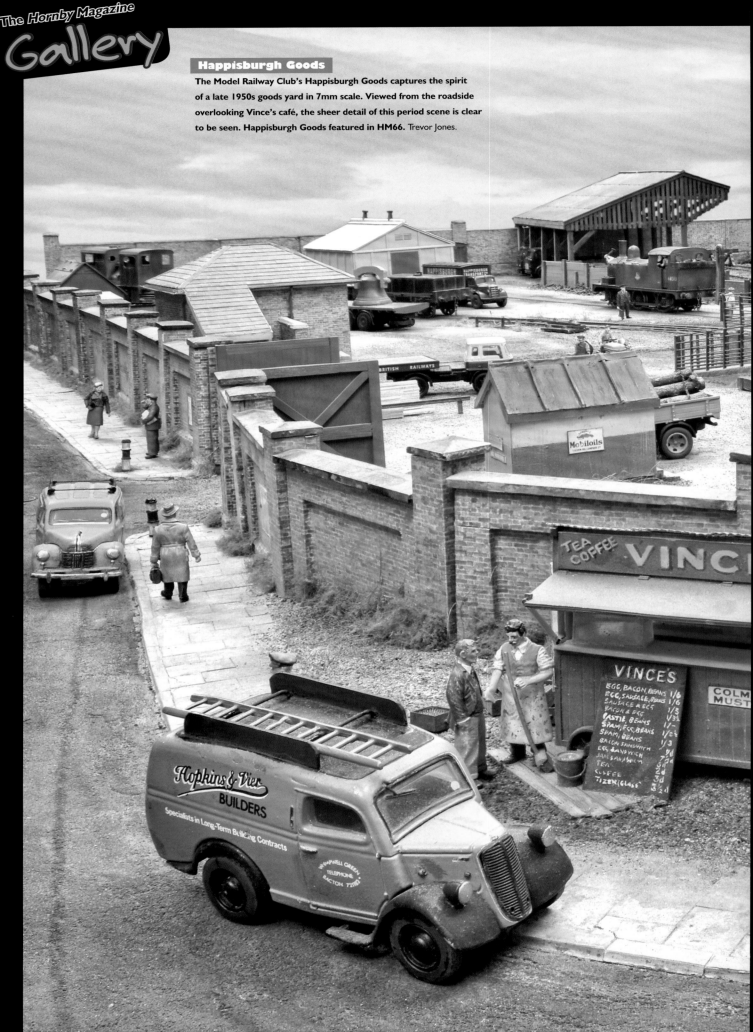

Happisburgh Goods

The Model Railway Club's Happisburgh Goods captures the spirit
of a late 1950s goods yard in 7mm scale. Viewed from the roadside
overlooking Vince's café, the sheer detail of this period scene is clear
to be seen. Happisburgh Goods featured in HM66. Trevor Jones.

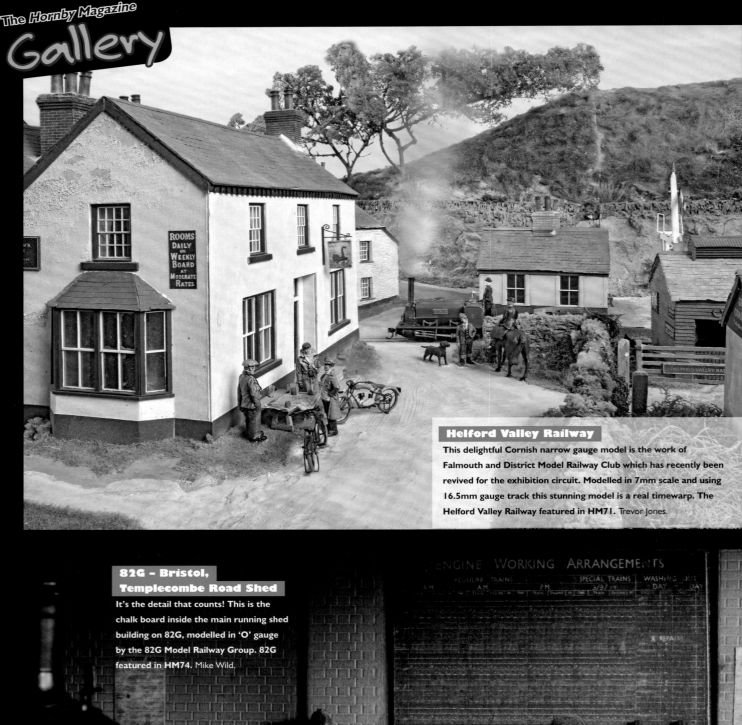

Helford Valley Railway

This delightful Cornish narrow gauge model is the work of Falmouth and District Model Railway Club which has recently been revived for the exhibition circuit. Modelled in 7mm scale and using 16.5mm gauge track this stunning model is a real timewarp. The Helford Valley Railway featured in **HM71.** Trevor Jones.

82G - Bristol, Templecombe Road Shed

It's the detail that counts! This is the chalk board inside the main running shed building on 82G, modelled in 'O' gauge by the 82G Model Railway Group. 82G featured in **HM74.** Mike Wild.

Horton Regis

Viewed through the stonework of the station buildings, a Metropolitan Railway 4-4-0T simmers in the platform at Horton Regis. Horton Regis featured in HM64 and models the a former LSWR terminus pre-1923. Trevor Jones.

Hobbs Row Halt

Proving that small is beautiful is Bob Vaughan's inspirational Hobbs Row Halt. Set on the dinner table as a centerpiece, in a style favoured by American modellers, this delightful narrow gauge layout is a feast of detail. Hobbs Row Halt featured in HM74. Trevor Jones.

Ingleton Sidings

Paul Allen's compact shunting layout, Ingleton Sidings, measures just 45in in length and 7in in width, yet its puzzle layout keeps it entertaining. Ingleton Sidings featured in **HM75**. Trevor Jones.

Tamerig Central

The Taunton Model Railway Group's 'home' set up for its award winning Bath Green Park model revolves around the impressive continuous run station called Tamerig Central. This massive railway complex featured in full in HM75. Trevor Jones.

Empingham

Modelling a Northamptonshire branch line in the 1950s, Empingham features one of the key traffic flows of the area – ironstone. An Ivatt '4MT' 2-6-0 shunts in the yard as a '4F' 0-6-0 draws into the loop at the station. Empingham featured in HM65. Trevor Jones.

Weydon Road

The busy main line station at Weydon Road echos to the sounds of a BR '4MT' 2-6-0 and a Bulleid rebuilt 'West Country' 4-6-2 as two trains pass at the station throat. This busy 'O' gauge layout feature in HM70. Trevor Jones.

GARTONS
SEED
MERCHANTS
EST.
1848

Southern
COMFORT

Paul Chetter describes a straightforward DCC sound installation into a Hornby 'Schools' 4-4-0 - a simple project for any modeller.

Maunsell 'Schools' 4-4-0
30936 *Cranleigh* leaves
Southampton Central
with the 12.00pm
Waterloo to Lymington
on August 25 1962. Mike
Fox/Rail Archive Stephenson.

Does DCC installation have to be complicated? Surely when we have so many DCC ready locomotives available off the shelf there are ways and means of keeping projects simple.

I am my own worst enemy when it comes to sound projects. I aim for the highest specification possible in all cases but, occasionally, I allow discretion to get the better of my valour, and Hornby's splendid 'Schools' 4-4-0 is a case in point. The way this model was designed makes adding smoke and working lamps, or putting the decoder or speaker inside the locomotive body very difficult indeed.

The 'Schools' has been available from Hornby in the past as a DCC sound fitted model. This was using a LokSound V4.0 decoder installed at the factory, but this version of the Maunsell 4-4-0 is now hard to come by. Having sourced a model I needed an alternative way of introducing the sounds of the real locomotives to this 'OO' gauge project.

Having conceded that adding DCC sound would be the extent of this conversion, my plan was to do so without modifying the model in any way, and the result is probably the simplest sound installation I've written about for Hornby Magazine so far, and is even completely reversible if needed.

Two screws and two tabs hold the tender body and chassis together. With these removed, the body can be raised at the front, the rear tabs released and the whole lifted clear.

There is a hole in the ballast weight which can easily accommodate a Zimo 12mm x 15 mm 'cube' speaker, the 8-pin DCC socket can be used as provided, and there is enough space on the underside of the coal bunker to take a pair of 'stay alive' capacitors wired in parallel.

Surprisingly for such a low profiled prototype, there is still sufficient space to fit a full sized 'OO' gauge sound decoder inside the 'Schools' tender too. I used a Zimo MX645R because it includes on-board control of the 'stay alive'

capacitors, but an ESU V4.0 would be an alternative if you are prepared to forego the capacitors.

The fitting instructions are simple. Connect the two purple wires to the speaker, solder the grey wire to the negative leg of each capacitor and the blue wire to the positives. Fully insulate these joints and any exposed electrical components. Remove the 8-pin blanking plug and replace with that of the decoder. Tidy up the wiring and replace the tender top, re-fixing the two retaining screws.

Insert the 4-pin plug from the locomotive into the tender socket near the drawbar, and the model is ready to run with no cutting, filing, drilling or grinding required.

The 'Schools' class 4-4-0s were something of a legend on the Southern Region putting impressive performances in on a daily basis as the head of express and stopping trains. The addition of sound to Hornby's excellent model of these three-cylinder locomotives really brings their character alive.

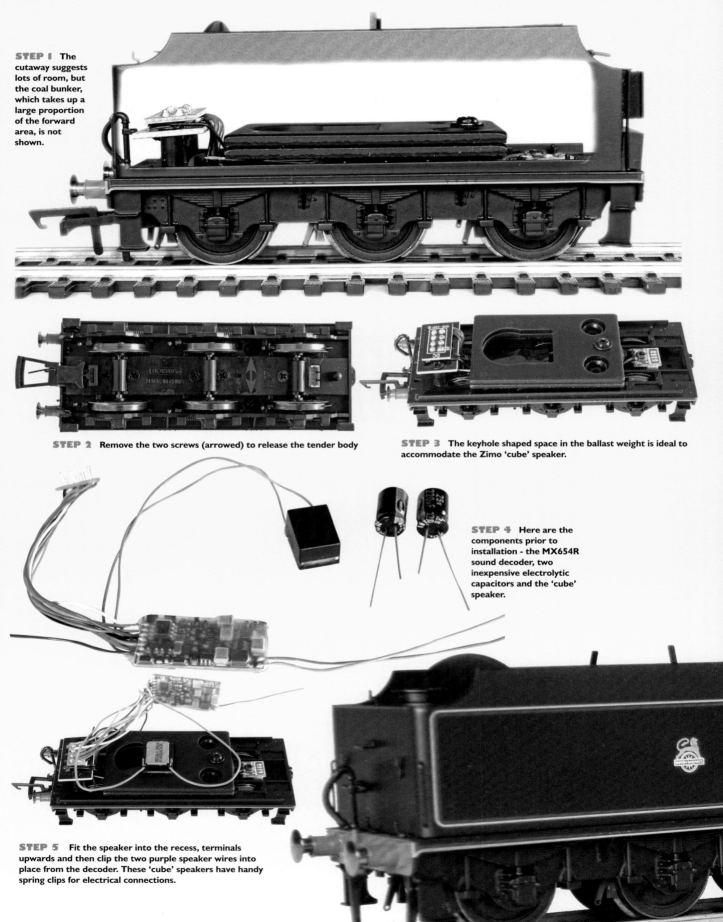

STEP 1 The cutaway suggests lots of room, but the coal bunker, which takes up a large proportion of the forward area, is not shown.

STEP 2 Remove the two screws (arrowed) to release the tender body

STEP 3 The keyhole shaped space in the ballast weight is ideal to accommodate the Zimo 'cube' speaker.

STEP 4 Here are the components prior to installation - the MX654R sound decoder, two inexpensive electrolytic capacitors and the 'cube' speaker.

STEP 5 Fit the speaker into the recess, terminals upwards and then clip the two purple speaker wires into place from the decoder. These 'cube' speakers have handy spring clips for electrical connections.

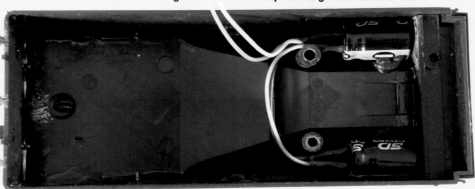

STEP 6 Shown here in a 'dry run', each capacitor nestles neatly between the tender bodyside and the underside of the coal bunker. A small blob of sticky mastic will hold them securely in place.

STEP 7 Plug in the decoder and tidy the wiring. I used mastic for this.

▶ **STEP 8** The capacitors are wired in parallel, and the soldered joints and any exposed wire insulated with shrink tubing. Re-assemble the tender body and chassis, re-fitting the two retaining screws.

STEP 9 The locomotive to tender wiring harness is plugged into the tender socket to complete the electrical circuits, and the model is ready to run.

▼ **STEP 10** With all of the sound decoder components neatly contained within the tender body of the 'Schools' this makes for a neat and simple installation which is quick to do too.

Rolling stock built from plastic kits can be mixed with ready to run wagons to introduce variety within the fleet. Careful weathering of both will disguise any differences in paint finish. This view shows 'Rudd' and 'Grampus' ballast wagons with various detail differences constructed from Parkside Dundas kits.

Starting
OUT IN KIT
CONSTRUCTION

Every newcomer to railway modelling should try at least one plastic rolling stock kit, says **Nigel Burkin**, who describes the essentials of plastic wagon kit construction in 'OO' gauge.

I t seems to me that many modellers believe that making a start in rolling stock kit construction is not worthwhile because of the growing range of off-the-shelf models in 'OO' and 'N' gauge. I take a different view and believe that building rolling stock kits is a rite of passage for all modellers. It is important on many levels, not only because of the immense satisfaction from completing something for oneself. Kit-built models introduce much needed variety to the layout too.

Paradoxically, one reason to invest time building rolling stock kits is the way that ready-to-run models are produced in batches. The Hornby 'Rudd' engineers wagon is hard to find in model shops because it was produced in batches. Once sold, that's it until the next run. The same applies to the 'Grampus' ballast wagon produced by Dapol. It may feature in the catalogue, but has a batch been produced recently?

The 'Grampus' is a case in point: I build Parkside Dundas 'Grampus' kits simply because I cannot find enough ready-to-run models for my layout operations. Furthermore, it is easier to work differences between individual wagons during construction.

Finally, there are always some wagons not available as ready-to-run models. Kit building may be the only way to obtain a model key to a layout theme.

The arguments for plastic rolling stock kit construction are compelling and I urge new modellers to try at least one! The buzz you will get from finishing it, even before painting, feels great. I have been building for years, but the feeling of deep satisfaction when completing a kit never goes away.

In this article, I share the basic techniques required to complete four-wheel plastic wagon kits using two similar wagons - the Parkside Dundas

Far right: The variety of wagons that can be built from rolling stock kits is quite vast. In this BR engineers wagon scene, there are four different kits representing five different wagons including Diagram 1/574 vacuum braked 'Grampus', two types of 'Rudd'; a 'Crab' and a Diagram 1/570 'Lamprey'! One 'Rudd' is a rebuilt air braked 'Grampus' whilst the other two represent complete rebuilds of HTV coal hopper wagons (ZBA).

Right: The 'Grampus' kit from Parkside Dundas is very comprehensive. It has optional parts for a refurbished air braked 'Grampus' variant called 'Rudd' before 'Rudds' were rebuilt from HTV coal hopper wagons.

Diagram 1/574 'Grampus' (Cat No. PC72) and the Chivers 'Crab' (RC445). Both are engineers wagons from the BR era and both are essential to my Southern Region project.

Key tools

To enjoy the satisfaction of building your own wagons, you do not need a huge array of expensive tools. You can equip a workbench with the correct tools for about £25, assuming you do not have them already for other modelling tasks.

When well cared for, tools should last for years of model building!

A real luxury for those planning to build more than a handful of plastic kits is a Xuron sprue cutter. Whilst one adds £10 to your tool shopping list, it makes the task of removing parts from sprues easier and may be used to cut soft wire too.

Consumables such as adhesives and filler should not add more than about £12 to the job of starting kit construction.

STEP-BY-STEP AN INTRODUCTION TO WAGON KIT CONSTRUCTION

STEP 1 Commence construction by cleaning up parts, removing them from the sprue and identifying the ones you need for your chosen wagon. The 'Grampus' kit has two types of end to choose from – one for a typical 'Grampus' and one for the 'Rudd'.

STEP 2 Xuron sprue cutters are relatively expensive, optional but very useful, especially when building more than a couple of wagons in one go. A protective sprue is snipped cleanly from the 'Grampus' wagon sides.

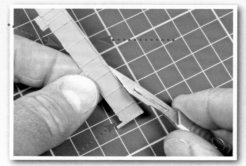

STEP 3 Moulding flash and ridges are pared from the edges of parts using a modelling knife blade.

STEP 4 The top of the wagon sides and ends, together with other components are finished by rubbing gently against grade 600 wet and dry paper.

STEP 5 Hard to reach areas are cleaned of moulding lines using wet and dry paper wrapped or glued to lolly sticks.

CONTINUED...

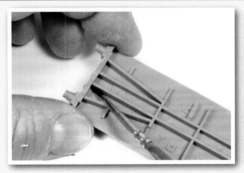

STEP 6 Assembly of the 'Grampus' starts by applying the ends to the floor. The floor sits on a shelf behind the headstocks.

STEP 7 When assembling the sides to the ends, note how the corners fit together to make a neat join.

STEP 8 Turning our attention to the Chivers 'Crab' wagon kit; note that the corner joins are designed to go together. They differ from the Parkside Dundas kit.

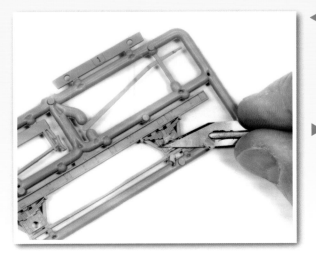

STEP 9 Some tasks are best completed with parts attached to the sprue. The oil axleboxes are replaced with roller bearing axle boxes in the 'Crab' wagon kit.

STEP 10 Many kits supply alternative parts for various details and I decided to apply roller bearing details to the 'Crab'.

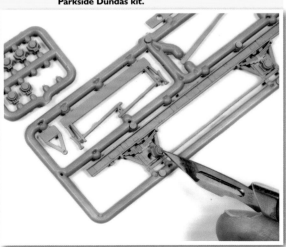

HOW TO GUIDES

KEY POINTS OF KIT CONSTRUCTION

- ● Always read the instructions carefully and look for optional parts in the kit and see if your chosen project requires them.
- ● Lay the kit parts out on the workbench and make sure nothing is missing.
- ● Clean delicate components of moulding flash before detaching them from the sprue to avoid breakage.
- ● Use reference photographs from books and the internet as reference if modelling specific variations of wagon.
- ● Special adhesives such as solvent cement should be used sparingly to avoid distorting kit components.
- ● When building a rake of wagons from plastic kits, consider building them in batches.
- ● For certain wagon types and kits it is sometimes easier to paint the wagon interior before assembly.

- ● Practice assembling the kit without adhesives or solvent cement to see how the parts fit together.
- ● Consider how you can improve the kit. Are there moulded details that can be replaced with cast metal components (buffers for example) and moulded handrails replaced with fine brass wire?
- ● Buy the best wheels you can afford. Quality turned metal wheelsets will go a long way towards ensuring that your finished wagon runs well.
- ● Make sure you have sharp modelling knife blades to hand. Blunt blades slip on plastic surfaces, make the project harder to do, can damage kit components and twist towards your hand and fingers.
- ● Leftover parts should be stored in a 'spares' box because you will always find a use for them in another project.

The list of these is simple: superglue, putty-style filler such as 'Squadron', solvent cement, pinpoint bearings, wheels, and couplings of your choice.

Given that most plastic kits are composed of styrene plastic, the best adhesive to use is solvent cement. It is a liquid which melts plastic which makes for a clean assembly. It should be used sparingly, is applied with a small clean paintbrush dedicated to the task and the application of excessive solvent should be avoided.

Very small amounts of solvent can be applied to a model with a micro brush when attaching fine details such as brake hangers, levers and door springs avoiding any stains on the components.

Look carefully at the label when choosing solvent cements. There are several types and those which will work on a wide variety of plastics including ABS and styrene are considered the best and if strongest. Some do not work on harder plastics such as ABS and will be less harsh. Whichever you choose, always use in a well ventilated area and replace the top of the bottle between applications or you will lose it through evaporation.

STEP-BY-STEP | AN INTRODUCTION TO WAGON KIT CONSTRUCTION ...CONTINUED

STEP 11 Do not fit the pinpoint bearings with CA glue. Use a spot of solvent cement applied with a small paintbrush instead so they can be adjusted if required.

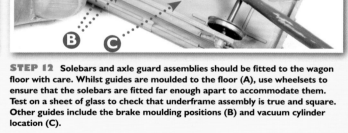

STEP 12 Solebars and axle guard assemblies should be fitted to the wagon floor with care. Whilst guides are moulded to the floor (A), use wheelsets to ensure that the solebars are fitted far enough apart to accommodate them. Test on a sheet of glass to check that underframe assembly is true and square. Other guides include the brake moulding positions (B) and vacuum cylinder location (C).

STEP 13 To be sure the pinpoint bearings fit the axle guards, drill out the openings with a 2mm drill fitted to a pin vice. The Parkside Dundas 'Grampus' is shown in this picture.

▶ **STEP 14** My choice of axlebox cover is chosen from the three supplied with the 'Grampus' kit and fitted over the pinpoint bearing using a tiny spot of solvent. Micro-brushes are perfect for applying small amounts of solvent.

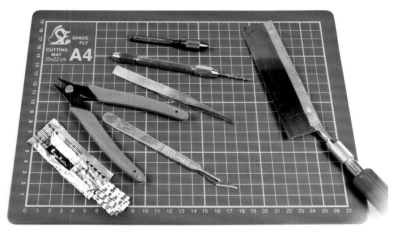

Other adhesives to consider are conventional cements such as Humbrol and UHU. I also like to have a special adhesive called Plasti-Zap to hand because it has many uses in adding metal parts to plastic models and is formulated to work on 'difficult' plastics. Don't apply it straight from the bottle. Place a spot on a small piece of kitchen foil and apply using a cocktail stick instead. This avoids the risk of flooding the model and ruining it completely!

Get stuck in...

There are numerous wagon kits available representing everything from everyday revenue-earning wagons to one-off vehicles built for specialist uses. They range from modern air braked vehicles to pre-grouping and steam era private owner wagons. You can refine your kits too by using other details such as transfers, buffers, couplings, tail lamps and brake pipes from third party companies.

Whatever you do, you can be sure that your creation will be unique and much more satisfying than relying solely on ready-to-run models to equip your layout.

Top left: A selection of tools used to build the kits demonstrated in this article including a Swan Morton scalpel handle and No. 10A blades, twist drills, pin vice and Xuron sprue cutters. Use a cutting mat to protect the table from modelling knife blades when detaching parts from the sprue.

Bottom left: Adhesives and solvents useful in plastic wagon kit construction. A putty filler such as 'Squadron' has uses in filling small imperfections in plastic mouldings. Use glues in well ventilated areas and store in a cool dry place.

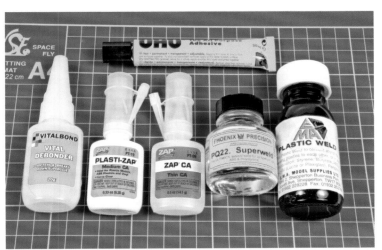

STEP 15 Underframe detailing follows including the fitting of V-hangers, brake levers and brake mouldings.

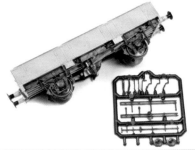

STEP 16 The 'Grampus' is shown equipped with 8-shoe clasp brakes (Diagram 1574) but no underframe baskets. I choose not to fit them because they prevent the fitting of No. 146 Kadee couplings.

STEP 17 Small details which need care in fitting to the correct side of this type of wagon in relation to the vacuum cylinder are the brake levers. Look for reference letters moulded on the underside of the floor which indicate the location of specific details.

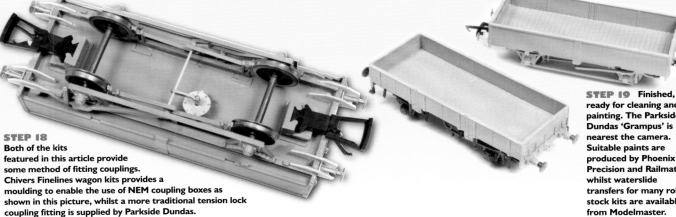

STEP 18 Both of the kits featured in this article provide some method of fitting couplings. Chivers Finelines wagon kits provides a moulding to enable the use of NEM coupling boxes as shown in this picture, whilst a more traditional tension lock coupling fitting is supplied by Parkside Dundas.

STEP 19 Finished, ready for cleaning and painting. The Parkside Dundas 'Grampus' is nearest the camera. Suitable paints are produced by Phoenix Precision and Railmatch whilst waterslide transfers for many rolling stock kits are available from Modelmaster.

Weathering
A PAIR OF 0-6-0s

I f ever there was one type of locomotive which summed up the steam era, it would be the 0-6-0. Thousands were built by all the railway companies before and after the 1923 grouping and many of those continued in service well into the BR era.

Two the subjects here are polar opposites when it comes to Southern Region 0-6-0s. On one hand we have the 'modern' Bulleid 'Q1' 0-6-0 introduced in 1942 and packing the same power as a Stanier 'Black Five' into a compact, rugged and easy to maintain design. On the other we have the Victorian era Wainwright 'C' class 0-6-0 which was introduced in 1900 by the South Eastern and Chatham Railway.

Both of these designs continued in service through the 1950s and into

The 0-6-0 was the lifeblood of freight work on British railways right through to the 1960s. **Mike Wild** tackles two Southern Region locomotives from completely different periods and gives them that 'in service' look.

the1960s with the last 'Q1' being withdrawn in 1966 and the last 'C' in 1963. Currently they are the source of ready-to-run models in 'OO' gauge from Hornby ('Q1') and Bachmann ('C'), but both feature one important and easily remedied flaw – their pristine finish.

As a weathering project these two models offer an interesting comparison in styles. The 'C' class tended to weather with a dusty finish, but many photographs of them in the 1950s and

early 1960s show them in fairly clean condition.

The 'Q1s' on the other hand tended to have more oil splattered over their wheels and motion while also seeing streaks of dirt running down the boiler casing from the beading along the top.

Both are excellent base models to work from and with subtle adjustments to the weathering process make for attractive and interesting projects which will bring new life to these models.

Weathered with a mixture of Humbrol and Lifecolor paints, the pristine finish of the original models is gone, but with a much more realistic weathering look being the end result.

STEP 1 Fresh from the box the 'Q1' from Hornby (left) and the 'C' class from Bachmann (right) are ideal candidates for weathering. The two classes weathered in subtly different ways.

STEP 2 Starting with the 'Q1' the first step is to invert the model. There is a lot of detail high up on the chassis which could easily be missed if it remained the right way up. The airbrush is an Iwata dual-action model and the first paint colour we're using is Lifecolor's ever versatile 'Frame Dirt'.

STEP 3 Starting around the front of the 'Q1' using thinned 'Frame Dirt', the area we target first is under the bufferbeam as this is easy to miss. Following this attention moves along the underside of the boiler casing covering the wheels and motion as we go.

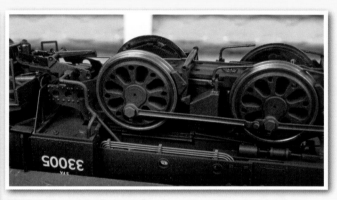

STEP 4 Around the firebox is fine pipework and the raised detail of the firebox itself low down in the chassis. A mist of 'Frame Dirt' in these areas helps to highlight the details and reveal their relief.

WHAT WE USED

Product	Cat No.
Humbrol black wash	AV0201
Humbrol gloss oil stain wash	AV0209
Humbrol thinners	AC7501
Humbrol white enamel wash	AV0202
Humbrol dark grey enamel wash	AV0204
Lifecolor 'Burned Rust' pigment	PG107
Lifecolor acrylic thinners	LC-THINNER-250
Lifecolor 'Frame Dirt'	UA719
Lifecolor Tensocrom smoke	TSC208

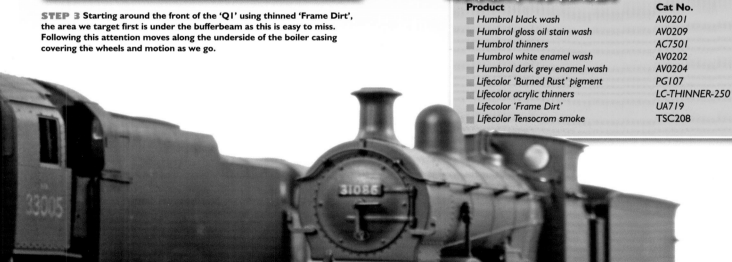

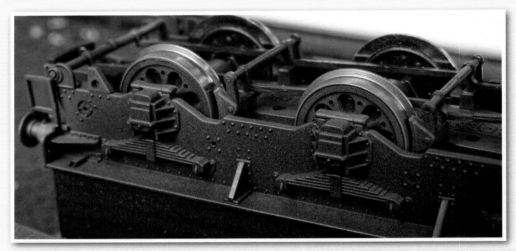

◄ **STEP 5** The tender underframe receives the same treatment, but don't forget to rotate the wheels so they are fully weathered.

▼ **STEP 6** Having turned the 'Q1' back onto its wheels the same colour is applied with the airbrush again, but from above now ensuring that sandboxes, the bottom of the smokebox and the lower tender bodysides all get a hint of 'Frame Dirt' on them.

STEP 8 Setting the 'Q1' to oneside we turned our attention to the 'C' class. From the box it is very black, with little relief in the paint finish.

STEP 7 More 'Frame Dirt' applied around the front end highlights the details of the lower part of the smokebox and the bufferbeam. This will all be blended in later in the process.

STEP 9 The underframe was treated in the same manner as the 'Q1' taking care to ensure that all of the wheels were weathered.

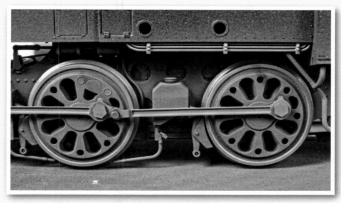

STEP 10 Back to the 'Q1' and both locomotives were put onto the track to rotate their wheels so any bits missed with the first pass could be tackled.

STEP 11 Moving onto the body of the two locomotives and the next colour used is Humbrol's new black wash enamel, again applied with an airbrush. It was added in vertical passes, building up the paint gradually to create the final effect.

STEP 12 To enhance the appearance of the axleboxes the black enamel wash was sprayed onto them giving them more texture.

STEP 13 However, it all still looks quite flat and needs relief and texture adding to the paint finish.

STEP 14 Using a flat brush lightly dampened with thinners, vertical streaks were brushed into the black base colour to suggest rain and dirt running down the sides of the locomotive from the beading. The process was repeated a couple of times to create the final look.

STEP 15 On the 'C' class the same basic paint finish was applied, making sure that the cab interior also got a dusting of paint to tone it down.

STEP 17 Taking the 'C' class a step further Humbrol's oil stain gloss enamel wash was airbrushed over the air pump on the boiler side as well as the coupling rod pins.

The 'C' class 0-6-0s were often seen in fairly clean condition and this model reflects that. The grey colour base colour to the weathering is typical of the period.

STEP-BY-STEP — WEATHERING A 'Q1' AND A 'C' CLASS

STEP 18 Having applied the same black onto the tender axleboxes as on the 'Q1' the oil stain wash was airbrushed over the top deepening the detail further.

STEP 19 The 'Q1s' had a tendency to throw oil around the wheels from the motion. To reflect this we used the Humbrol oil stain wash spraying it in light coats to build up the effect. As with the 'C' class the coupling rods and coupling rods pins were also targeted together with the pipework and reversing rod underneath the boiler.

STEP 20 To represent grease on the bufferheads a very light application of the oil stain colour through the airbrush built up a neat effect.

STEP 23 To add a more subtle and grey final finish to the two models we used Humbrol's dark grey enamel wash, again applied with an airbrush. Streaks were added into this top coat with a flat brush again before a final light spray over with the dark grey wash.

STEP 21 At the front end the couplings of both locomotives were given a light blow over with the oil stain wash together with the bufferheads.

STEP 24 To add a little character below the frames, the side of the firebox through the circular cut outs in the frames of the 'Q1' were weathered with a touch of Lifecolor 'Burned Rust' pigment.

STEP 25 The footplate and lower part of the smokebox were also treated to a little touch of 'Burned Rust' followed by DCC Concepts' 'Ultramarine Black' below the smokebox door.

STEP 22 The pipework on the right hand side of the 'Q1' lends itself beautifully to Humbrol's oil stain wash, applied in tiny quantities by airbrush.

STEP 26 The 'C' class meanwhile received the same dark grey wash applied over the top of the main body colour adding further depth to its finish. Streaks were added in the same way as before.

STEP 28 The finished effect gives a line, but with a feathered edge. This was further blended into the body colours with more of Humbrol's dark grey wash.

STEP 27 Having seen a photograph of 31481 with heavy limescale stains on its boiler, we decided to replicate this too. First a card mask was made up by cutting two different sized slots into it. This was then held over the locomotive side so that Humbrol white enamel wash could be sprayed over it.

USEFUL LINKS

■ **Lifecolor paints and pigments**
www.airbrushes.com

■ **Humbrol paints**
www.humbrol.com

■ **DCC Concepts powders**
www.dccconcepts.com

Twelve Trees Junction
THE SCENERY

Scenery is all about breathing believable life into a model railway and with an urban scene that can be a fascinating challenge. **Mike Wild** reveals how the backdrop to Twelve Trees Junction developed from flat baseboards into a detailed and evolving miniature world.

A rebuilt Bulleid 'West Country' 4-6-2 leads an express towards Twelve Trees Junction as a Maunsell 'King Arthur' 4-6-0 heads North towards the capital. The grass land in the foreground is to be further detailed.

Looking back through previous *Hornby Magazine Yearbook* project layouts, Twelve Trees Junction really stands out. Not because it is Southern Region and not because of its size, but for the simple reason that it models an urban scene.

St Stephens Road (Yearbook No. 4) and Topley Dale (Yearbook No. 5) followed a broadly similar pattern, but set in different areas with defining features. However, they were both country layouts which meant a limited number of buildings and structures were required to complete them.

Twelve Trees Junction on the other hand is a totally different beast. Buildings and structures are the main theme of the scenery while greenery takes a back seat by comparison. This kind of urban backdrop is a great pleasure to create, but it does become much more involved

than a country scene. Even now we haven't fully completed work on Twelve Trees' scenery with a large amount of weathering and bedding-in required before the layout makes its exhibition debut.

Starting point

Twelve Trees Junction started as an almost blank canvas in terms of scenery. The baseboards were entirely bare except for one feature – the platforms. These had been built previously and were the only element of the original Project 12 plan to be kept.

The platforms are 6ft long and will accommodate a six coach train. Using these original platforms the new trackplan offers four platform faces: Platform 1 is the bay, Platforms 2 and 3 are on the through main lines while Platform 4 is to the rear of the station

and is used as a loop for slow trains to be held.

The platforms are built using Peco Southern Region style concrete platform facings with plasticard spacers and a plasticard top. To enhance the platform surface the plasticard was skimmed with decorators filler to create the final surface which adds a little bit of texture and, in turn, more realism.

With the platforms already in place our first port of call was to begin mocking up an arrangement for buildings. Have decided on an urban scene we knew we would need a lot of buildings and began by placing a selection of Skaledale shops together in a row behind the station. At the same time we were visualising how a selection of low relief buildings – see pages 46-49 – would work along the back of the layout beyond the skew bridge.

Initially these buildings were placed onto the flat baseboard, but even at this point we knew that they would need to be raised above the level of the railway. This also meant sourcing bridges to go across each end of the layout to create a 'start' and 'end' point for the scenic section.

Rise and fall

A standout feature of the baseboards for this project is their differing levels. We wanted the land around the railway to rise and fall below the level of the trackbed and this has been achieved through two methods.

At the station end of Twelve Trees the road and town is above the level of the railway with the station appearing to sink into the ground between retaining walls. This area has been built up using readily available polystyrene home insulation sheeting. This material, while not exactly cheap, is an excellent medium, being lightweight, strong and easily cut to shape to fit specific areas.

Our roadway is 75mm above the baseboard level around the station formed of a 50mm thick and 25mm thick layer of polystyrene. These layers are bonded together with rapid setting 'no more nails' type adhesive which provides a strong and resilient joint between the materials.

With the base of the roadway built

the Skaledale buildings which were to form the actual street were repositioned on top of the polystyrene to get a new impression of how the completed layout might look. It is always advantageous to position buildings loose on a layout during early construction as it allows changes to be made at any time. For example, we re-ordered the buildings behind the station several times until we found the best arrangement.

The street scene along the back of the layout is punctuated by the skew bridge - see pages 50-53 - before continuing along at full height to the end of the second full baseboard. At this point, halfway along the scenic section, the medium for the road surface changes to 6mm MDF to allow a hill to be built leading the road below railway level. It drops to 30mm below the railway and ultimately ends up at a London Transport bus depot which sits in the shadows of the 4ft long carriage shed.

With all the groundwork for the roads established the next step was to cover them with a suitable surface. Our medium of choice is artists mounting board which is available in a variety of pre-coloured finishes. At 2mm thick it is strong too, but also easy to bend to shape to follow contours. To make all the roads on Twelve Trees we used two A1 size sheets of grey/green mounting

WHAT WE USED
DETAILING

Product	Manufacturer	Cat No.
Cable drums	Bachmann Scenecraft	44-504
Caged gas bottles	Bachmann Scenecraft	44-537
Oil drums	Knightwing	B003
Pallets	Faller, Gaugemaster	180612
Speed restriction signs	Eckon	EA7
Pratt Truss gantry	Ratio	478
Signal arms and poles	Ratio	476
Ground signals	Ratio	465
Telegraph poles	Ratio	452
70mm street lamps	TrainSave	TSV200
Telephone box	Hornby Skaledale	R8580
Postbox	Hornby Skaledale	R8579
Platform benches	Hornby Skaledale	R8674
Platform trolleys	Skaledale	R8676
Gas lamps	DCC Concepts	DML-LMSG
Trainspotters	Bachmann Scenecraft	36-401
Businessmen	Bachmann Scenecraft	36-040
Relay boxes	Wills	SS85/SS88

WHAT WE USED
GROUND COVER

Product	Manufacturer	Cat No.
Plaster bandage	Gaugemaster	GM100
Fine blended green turf	Woodland Scenics	WT1349
Light green coarse turf	Woodland Scenics	T1363
Olive green coarse turf	Woodland Scenics	T1362
Static grass, 4.5mm autumn	International Models	004-23
Static grass, 6.5mm autumn	International Models	006-33
Static grass, 4.5mm winter	International Models	004-24
Static grass, 6.5mm winter	International Models	006-34
Light green fine leaf foliage	Woodland Scenics	WF1132
Olive green fine leaf foliage	Woodland Scenics	WF1133

USEFUL LINKS

- **Woodland Scenics**
  www.bachmann.co.uk
- **International Models**
  www.internationalmodels.net
- **Gaugemaster**
  www.gaugemaster.com
- **Hatton's**
  www.ehattons.com

Right: During the early stages of construction a Bulleid designed 2-EPB EMU is about to be overtaken by a 'Merchant Navy' 4-6-2. To the right is the EMU carriage shed while below sits the London Transport bus depot site.

Far right: To settle the railway into the town the road was raised above the level of the trackbed. One of the features under development is this repair garage and sales yard.

board, all cut to shape with a craft knife. This was then fixed to the previous polystyrene or MDF structure with PVA wood glue and left to set.

The final addition to the road surfaces at this point was a pavement. This is built using Wills York paving kits which contain straight and corner sections of pavement. These neatly moulded plastic sections were cut from their sprues, spray painted with primer and then glued

in place with contact adhesive. A finishing touch was to apply a wash of Humbrol No 28 stone colour to represent mortar in the joints between paving slabs.

This rise and fall of the roadway has given the backdrop to Twelve Trees an interesting character and it is further enhanced by the scenery at the front of the layout. In front of the carriage sheds and main lines an 8ft long section of green belt land has been built – again

for further detailing in the future – which falls away from the railway towards the front of the layout. This was built with inspiration from the Southampton Model Railway Society's 4mm scale model of Romsey and also to become a vantage point for photography.

Like the roadbed around the station, the ground in front of the railway here is made from polystyrene insulation sheets. Using 25mm thick sheets glued

To add a little extra detail we used Evergreen 2mm square plastic strip to model a concrete lintel between the top of the wall and the bottom of the parapet.

The method adopted for Twelve Trees Junction is relatively quick to construct, particularly once the design was established, and the result is a good looking and detailed retaining wall as an immediate backdrop to the railway.

However, even with the retaining wall built there was more to do. We had decided on an engineer's brick colour theme for the retaining walls on the layout which meant a three stage colouring process for every section of wall. After building a section it was spray painted with ordinary grey car primer as a base colour. This was followed by a wash of Humbrol No. 28 thinned down with thinners to represent the mortar course and finally dry brushing of the brick faces with Humbrol blue grey No. 27 to complete the paint scheme.

To fix the retaining walls in place we

Above: Capturing an impressive South London scene a 'Brighton Belle' EMU thunders through the junction while a BR 'Standard Four' 4-6-0 waits in the platforms with a parcels working.

Left: In the early stages of the build a 'Merchant Navy' pauses at Twelve Trees Junction. At this point the various components of the road and bridge were being tested and checked.

to the timber frame with 'no more nails' type adhesive the polystyrene has been shaped and then covered with plaster bandage to create a solid and realistic landform in front of the railway.

Retaining walls
One of the biggest single projects for Twelve Trees Junction has been the development of the retaining wall which runs the full 16ft length of the scenic

section! This was a mammoth task with the whole wall being built using Wills brick sheets from scratch.

The height of the roadway, 75mm above the baseboard, is the same height as a single Wills brick sheet and also neatly corresponds with the height of the bridges at each end of the layout. Sheets were then cut into strips horizontally to form the parapet walls and vertically to form the buttresses.

The station forecourt has been finished with a layer of decorator's filler to give it a textured surface. Detailing including a telephone box, packages, vehicles and more.

used both 'no more nails' type adhesive and contact adhesive depending on the surface they were to be fixed to. The completed walls offer an impressive backdrop to the railway and really help to enhance the urban feeling of the model.

Ground cover

With the railway taking such a prominent position on Twelve Trees Junction the style of ground cover is limited on this layout. The most significant feature is ballast which covers more than half of the baseboard surface area. This is Woodland Scenics medium and fine grade blended grey ballast mixed together and applied with diluted PVA wood glue as detailed in the feature on pages 14-22 of this Yearbook.

A new material for *Hornby Magazine*'s layouts is chinchilla dust. This is an excellent material for representing gravel paths and yards and we have made use of this along the front of the layout to suggest a walking route for staff alongside the trackbed. In addition it has been used in the yard of the garage above the station.

However, beyond the railway there is still scope for detailing ground cover. We used three main products on the layout – Woodland Scenics fine blended green turf, Woodland Scenics fine leaf foliage and MiniNatur autumn and winter coloured static grasses.

The main area of green land is to the front of the layout, an area which is due to be further detailed in the future. After allowing the plaster bandage to set it was

painted brown with poster paint to give the grassland a suitable base colour. Neat PVA glue was then spread over this and covered with fine blended green turf to provide a first layer of grass. Once this had dried the excess was brushed off and collected for reuse.

To apply the first layer of static grass a 70:30 mixture of PVA glue and water was mixed and brushed over the top of the blended green turf to allow the MiniNatur grasses to be applied using a Noch GrasMaster. To make the most of these products Autumn and Winter shades were mixed together in the GrasMaster in 4.5mm and 6.5mm lengths for added variation.

Once this layer had dried a second layer of static grass was applied after brushing on a coat of 50:50 PVA glue and

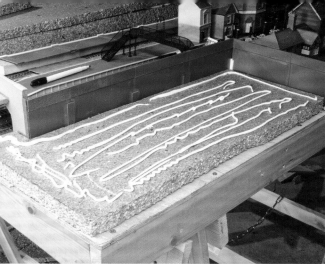

Top: To assemble the raised road we first glued together blocks of polystyrene insulation, 25mm thick in this case, which had previously been cut to shape. The adhesive is a 'no more nails' type product.

Middle: Three layers of 25mm polystyrene were used for the road. The plastic walling shows the end height for the 'ground'.

Below: To finish off the roads artists mounting card was used for the surfaces detailed with Wills York paving kits for the pavements. The mounting card was glued to the polystyrene base with PVA wood glue.

water. At the same time more of the Woodland Scenics fine blended green turf was sprinkled into the glue to give further depth to the scenery.

The finishing touches for the large grass areas were further detailing with layers of coarse and fine turfs to represent feeds and shrubs growing up through the grass. This was done by spraying Humbrol enamel matt varnish onto the now dried static grass, dusting on layers of turf, sealing them and repeating the process. In small quantities Woodland Scenics flowering foliage was rubbed to separate the colour from its mesh before yellow and purple flower heads were sprinkled on in limited amounts. These help to break up the green colouring of the grass while also suggesting small flowers growing in the grass.

Woodland Scenics fine leaf foliage has been used across the layout. This is an ideal material for bedding in buildings and filling small voids and it offers a highly realistic finish at the end. This material has been used along the footings of the retaining walls to suggest small bushes growing up the brickwork as well as to bed in the platform around the bay lines.

Detailing

The detailing of a model railway is something we really enjoy – another of those tasks which is totally absorbing and one which really makes a difference as to how a model looks.

The first area of the layout to be tackled was the station. Here DCC Concepts lamps were fitted by drilling 2.5mm holes through the platform surface, while Hornby Skaledale platform benches have been selected to provide seating for waiting passengers. Added to this if you look closely you will see baggage trolleys, a selection of tail lamps by one of the platform lamps alongside the bay platform and a collection of figures. The figures are from the Scenecraft range and include businessmen waiting for trains and Bachmann's recently introduced pack of trainspotters positioned at the best vantage point to watch all movements at the junction.

Outside the station the frontage has been detailed with vehicles, bicycles, a telephone box and postbox plus a collection of parcels waiting for onward

Top: To make the hill a sheet of 6mm MDF was cut to fit the area available. This material is flexible enough to be bent to shape without any force – just simply screwed down at each end.

Above: With the brick retaining wall taking shape the changes in levels become more apparent. The walling is awaiting painting in this view.

Middle right: To make the foreground scenery more polystyrene was used. This was fixed in place with 'no more nails' to the baseboard frame.

Bottom right: On the platform the first detail elements to be added were the station lamps. We used DCC Concepts gas lamps in a matching colour theme to the LBSCR colours of the station buildings.

movement by road after delivery to the station by rail. This is an area which will receive further detailing before Twelve Trees Junction makes its exhibition debut in 2014.

Along the back of the station you will notice a collection of sleepers and rails bedded into the ballast. These have been left here to suggest a former siding which has been removed and offers a little character which is slowly being overtaken by foliage.

On the roads behind the railway lamps from the TrainSave range have been installed on the pavements together with telegraph poles while a selection of suitable road vehicles, including the all important London Transport buses, has

been spread along the layout.

At the end of the platforms there are the two signal gantries, both built from Ratio's Pratt Truss gantry kits (see pages 44-45) while a Ratio Southern Railway concrete hut also stands at the platform end. A closer look also reveals a speed restriction sign, assembled from the Eckon kit, making sure that drivers are aware of the 50mph limit through the station.

Behind the junction is Twelve Trees Junction signalbox. This is detailed with relay boxes outside together with a collection of cable drums which stand next to the mess room for the EMU depot. A small concrete hut is here too together with a selection of caged

gas bottles (Bachmann Scenecraft) plus pallets by Faller and oil drums from Knightwing. Further relay boxes from the Wills kits also stand here to control the complex pointwork at the junction.

As the main line continues there are speed restriction signs for trains taking the junction heading South and for trains heading North to London plus a ground signal for movements to and from the carriage sidings.

The future

Like every layout Twelve Trees Junction is far from being finished, but it is largely complete. It presents a developing, but detailed model railway which shows just how much can be accomplished in a

limited time. From start to finish we had just 12 weeks to get the layout to this point, but that does leave a long job list to tackle over the coming months.

Twelve Trees Junction is set to make its exhibition debut at Hornby Magazine's Great Electric Train Show in October 2014 at the Heritage Motor Centre, Warwickshire, by which time we will have completed detailing the street scenes, weathering the track, adding more texture to the grass and finished off a number of other small detailing jobs.

Naturally we'll also be working on the rolling stock, but to find out more about the trains which will run on Twelve Trees Junction turn to page 112 now…

Air-smoothed Bulleid 'West Country' 4-6-2 34042 *Dorchester* **slows to a stop at Twelve Trees Junction with a London bound express.**

Bachmann released the first production samples of its version of pioneer diesels 10000 and 10001 in September offering the third, and most affordable, ready-to-run 'OO' gauge model of the LMS twins.

Each year, manufacturers produce a multitude of new locomotives, carriages, wagons and accessories and we always look forward to the new announcements and subsequent catalogues. Then all of us modellers spend ages poring over each page, mentally planning a strategy for the coming 12-18 months, and how much it is likely to cost!

I love nothing more than popping in to my local model shop and immersing myself in the range of model railway items on display. This, my local shopkeeper explains, is just 40% of what he has in stock as the shop is just not big enough to display everything! Hence, signs abound to the effect, if you can't see what you're after – just ask!

This past year has seen its fair share of new announcements and product releases, although in some quarters the release plan has faltered and a number of products have been delayed in the manufacturing process. The effects of this have been seen most by Hornby which announced delays into 2014 for a large number of planned catalogue items. Despite this the Margate based manufacturer has produced several stand

In *Hornby Magazine's* annual review of the year's highlights, **Mark Chivers** revisits the models that made the past 12 months so enthralling.

out new models in the past 12 months including five new steam locomotives and the 2-BIL EMU.

The delays in release may seem inconvenient, but this has meant that those products that have been released enjoy more breathing space and it allows us to budget more effectively and spread the cost of our hobby.

October 2012

We start our review where the last one left off, hot on the heels of Bachmann's stunning 'OO' model of the Midland Blue Pullman, the company also

revealed its latest exclusive 'OO' model for the National Railway Museum at Barrow Hill Roundhouse – the Great Central Railway 'Improved Director' 4-4-0 506 *Butler Henderson*. Whilst not a surprise given that Bachmann was producing models of the 'D11/1' and 'D11/2' 4-4-0s for the main catalogue range, this locomotive with its detail differences would remain exclusive to the NRM.

Hornby released the first of its new range of Thompson non-corridor coaches in 'OO,' all finished in BR plain carmine livery with straw

coloured lettering. The first three vehicles included a non-corridor Brake Third (E87228E), non-corridor Third (E82798E) and semi-corridor Lavatory Composite (E88512E).

In 'N' gauge Dapol released its model of the Gloucester Class 122 single car diesel multiple unit. This finely detailed new model looked good and ran well and was available in BR green (with whiskers or small yellow panel) BR blue, BR blue and grey and Network SouthEast colours. The N Gauge Society released its latest ready-to-run model in the form of the LMS Inspection saloon. A much-requested model, it was produced by Bachmann.

Dapol also impressed with its first step into 'O' gauge with the release of the RCH seven-plank open wagon

with end doors (Edinburgh Collieries) and RCH eight-plank open with fixed ends (BR grey).

October also saw *Hornby Magazine* unveil details of its latest 'OO' gauge model – the BR diesel brake tender. The new model is based on the round topped versions introduced in 1964-1965 and will feature Gresley pattern bogies, NEM coupling pockets, scale 14.4mm diameter wheels and sprung buffers.

November 2012

November saw the long-awaited 'OO' Hornby Gresley 'B17'

4-6-0, with review models of 2800 *Sandringham* in LNER lined apple green and 61637 *Thorpe Hall* in BR green with early crests landing on the editor's desk. *Hornby Magazine* also announced it was to produce a limited edition model of 'B17/6' 61662 *Manchester United* in weathered BR lined green with late crests.

Bachmann launched its Wainwright 'C' class 0-6-0 to high acclaim, with the SECR lined green version

Golden Age Models stunning 'O' gauge 'Merchant Navy' was one the highlights of the year.

selling out very quickly. The utilitarian appearance of the prototype was captured well by Bachmann. Versions in Southern black and BR black were also available. The Model Centre (TMC) of North Yorkshire released its 'OO' gauge Mk 1 horsebox.

Bachmann followed up its 'OO' benchmark model of the six-car Midland Blue Pullman with an equally impressive 'N' gauge version. Displaying all the hallmarks of its bigger brother, this iconic train touched down just in time for the Warley National Model Railway Exhibition.

Staying with 'N' gauge, Dapol continued its programme of releases with the Class 27 diesel. This followed the high standard of the Class 26 before it and consigned the oversized Minitrix versions to the scrapyard after all these years!

There was plenty of news in November too – Kernow Model Railway Centre announced it was to venture into 'O' gauge territory with a version of its '0298' 2-4-0WT, whilst Heljan confirmed its first general release foray into the steam market in 'OO' with plans for a Gresley 'O2' 2-8-0. Heljan also announced the Class 05 diesel shunter and original condition Class 26. At the NEC the Danish company showcased the latest pre-production samples of its

eagerly anticipated 'O' gauge Class 40 together with all the latest 'OO' samples such as the AC Cars railbus, Class 16 and original condition 'Baby Deltic'.

Meanwhile Bachmann's display at the NEC featured a host of new tooling samples including the first shots of the GWR 'Dukedog' 4-4-0, LMS 10000, the updated Class 40 and much more.

Dapol revealed that it was producing three new 'O' gauge models – a VEA, HEA and HAA – but it was less good news for Hornby, which confirmed that some items from its 2012 catalogue were being held over to 2013.

December 2012

December saw Bachmann deliver its 'OO' Fowler Midland Compound 4-4-0s, capturing the lines and shape just right. The wheels looked superb – some of the best we'd seen. Our LMS plain black liveried review model ran faultlessly and looked every inch just like the real thing. Making the news, Olivia's Trains released images of its new EM2 and Dapol announced its intention to produce the Class 121 and 122 diesel 'bubble' cars in its 'OO' range.

Just before Christmas Hornby unveiled its plans for the coming year with the 2013 range release on December 17. Highlights included BR '8P' 4-6-2 71000 *Duke of Gloucester*, Gresley 'P2' 2-8-2

Above: Olivia's Trains 'OO' gauge EM2 electric.

Below: Bringing new choice for GWR heavy freight trains was Hornby's GWR '42XX' 2-8-0T – one of three heavy freight tank engines produced by the manufacturer in 2013.

2001 *Cock O' The North*, a Churchward 'Star' 4-6-0, a new Collett 'Hall' 4-6-0 and the SR 2-BIL electric multiple unit in various liveries. For something slightly different, Hornby also revealed plans for the four-wheel Sentinel diesel industrial shunter.

30 new liveries on existing steam locomotive toolings were also unveiled including a special limited edition series of six LNER 'A4' locomotives to celebrate The Great Gathering planned for 2013. Twelve new liveries on existing diesel models were also promised including the Class 67 featuring the special Queen's Diamond Jubilee silver livery for the Hornby Collector's Club members.

A new range of Mk 1 coaches was announced for the Railroad range featuring a CK, SK and BSK in BR maroon and BR chocolate and cream colours and three new wagons were also promised including a BR 12ton 'Blue Spot' fish van, LMS/BR four-wheel CCT parcels van and a GWR shunter's truck.

Hornby's RailMaster computer software was also set for expansion with a new app for use on mobile phones and tablets and the promise of a new black box to replace the Elite called E-Link.

January 2013

The New Year started with a bump as two big releases arrived on the review desk –

the ink on the announcement of one had barely just dried!

First up was the Dapol Class 52 'Western' in 'OO' gauge, a type which has had a chequered history in model form over the years. No need to worry on that score with this model though, Dapol had clearly done its homework. The peak above the cab windows and the shelf below all looked good. A selection of BR maroon, green and blue-liveried versions together with a raft of limited editions were also available.

The second arrival was one that had only been revealed just before Christmas – the 2-BIL EMU. This model had been worked on quietly during the previous year and plans were in place to ensure it would be available during the early part of 2013. It was the first of Hornby's 'design clever' models and demonstrated what

Top: As well as the original air-smoothed 'Merchant', Golden Age released an equally fine model of the rebuilt locomotives for 'O'.

Above: Bachmann's new 'OO' gauge Midland '4F' 0-6-0.

Right: **Hornby's
Thompson 'O1' 2-8-0
was well received,
arriving in November
2012.**

Below: **Dapol's 'N'
gauge Class 27.**

the company was capable of producing at a more affordable price. Three versions were available, in SR olive green and two BR green versions – one as currently preserved by the NRM. Such was the popularity that another run had to be hastily arranged with the factory in China!

New from Dapol in 'N' gauge was the eagerly anticipated GWR Collett '2884' 2-8-0. Our two GWR liveried examples, 2884 in GWR green and 2892 in GWR green with 'shirtbutton' crests ran faultlessly and proved to be exceptionally good runners.

Meanwhile, Hornby International surprised with its announcement of an 'N' gauge version of the 'Brighton Belle' EMU through its Arnold brand. Later in the year Hornby confirmed it would be going ahead and be available exclusively via its own website.

February 2013

Hornby's 'OO' model of the GWR '42XX' arrived, the first time that the GWR's 2-8-0Ts had been produced as a ready-to-run locomotive. Two versions were released in GWR 'shirtbutton' green and BR black with large early crests, and it was clear Hornby had done a lot of research to recreate the overall look and feel of the design.

Also from Hornby came the first of its mainstream 'OO' Gresley 'B17/6' models, 61650 *Grimsby Town* in BR lined green with late crests. *Hornby Magazine's* limited edition model of 61662 *Manchester United* in late BR weathered green livery followed soon after.

After several years of waiting, Kernow Model Rail Centre's 'OO' gauge model of the Class 205 'Thumper' diesel-electric multiple unit arrived. Manufactured by Bachmann, several versions were produced including one featuring original engine room louvres and warning whistle (1108 in BR green) and one with later revised engine room louvres and air horns (1115 in BR green with orange 'V' and others in later period liveries).

In 'O' gauge, Heljan released its new model of the Class 31 diesel. Available in three liveries – BR green with small yellow warning panels, BR blue with twin double arrows and BR blue with single central double arrow – it captured the look and size of the real locomotives really well.

Bachmann's 'OO' GWR 'Modified Hall' 4-6-0 received an upgrade with a new DCC ready chassis featuring an 8-pin DCC decoder socket. Our review sample was of 7903 *Foremarke Hall* in BR lined black with early crest which ran as well as expected, although the batch was later recalled by Bachmann owing to a missing component on the body.

In the news section this month, Heljan released images of its forthcoming 'O' gauge AC Cars railbus, Bachmann

announced an updated version of its 6-pin (Cat No. 36-558A) and 21-pin DCC decoders (36-557) as part of an ongoing programme of improvement, and Rail Exclusive unveiled plans to commission more 'OO' gauge ViTrains Class 47s, this time in BR large logo blue livery as 47617 *University of Stirling* and 47636 *Sir John De Graeme*.

March 2013

Excitement mounted as Olivia's Trains EM2 Co-Co express electric locomotive arrived in the office for review. Announced at the same time as the EM1, this stunning 'OO' model exceeded expectations in both detail and performance. Our review sample was BR gloss black as 27000 with three different formats available – DCC ready,

DCC fitted and DCC sound.

A surprise package contained Heljan's 'OO' gauge Class 128 diesel parcels unit, another superb model which looked brilliant whispering along the test track.

The big news for the month was the annual Bachmann catalogue launch which included four new steam 'OO' locomotives – a Stanier '5MT' 2-6-0, Johnson '1F' 0-6-0T, LBSCR Billinton 'E4' 0-6-2T and a GWR '64XX' 0-6-0PT. Various liveries of each were announced together with 27 new versions of the existing steam locomotives in the range. For diesel modellers, Class 24/1 and Class 43 locomotives were set to join the fold as will a new model of the Wickham Type 27 engineers trolley in 'OO'.

The carriage and wagon department

Above left: Bachmann's 'OO' gauge SECR 'C' 0-6-0.

Above right: Hornby's long awaited 'B17' 4-6-0 touched down in November 2012. This is the 'B17/6' variant.

Top: Kernow's eagerly anticipated Class 205 DEMU made its debut after five years in the making.

Middle: 'N' gauge came right up to date with the General Electric Class 70.

Bottom: Adding further to the range of hydraulics for 'N' gauge is the NBL Class 22 from Dapol.

saw six new coach designs for 'OO' – retooled LNER Thompson carriages, a Hawksworth-design autocoach, SECR 'Birdcage' stock, LMS Inspection saloons, BR Mk 1 POT TPO stowage vans and a new range of Mk 2F carriages which will also include the BR Mk 2F DBSO. Seven new goods wagons were announced for 'OO' too including new models of the BR 21ton grain hopper, 12ton pipe wagon, BR Tube wagon, War Dept 'Warflat', GWR shunters truck, 20ton four-wheel tanker and the 45ton Class B TTA tank wagon with conical ends.

In 'N' gauge, Bachmann's Graham Farish brand announced five new steam locomotives – the GWR '64XX' 0-6-0PT and 'Castle' 4-6-0, SR 'N' 2-6-0, and an LMS Fairburn 2-6-4T and '4F' 0-6-0.

Three new diesel locomotives are planned for the scale too – the Class 25/1, Class 25/2 and Class 47/7 in a selection of liveries, as well as 27 other new versions of existing models. BR built Hawksworth coaching stock and

Mk 2F air conditioned carriages lead the way in terms of coaching stock, whilst the Maunsell Van B bogie luggage van and Maunsell four-wheel passenger luggage van are new in terms of parcels stock. Four new wagons are also being introduced - the Midland 20ton brake van, BR 12ton pipe wagon, Southern Railway ventilated vans and the BR CovHop.

April 2013

Hornby completed its 'OO' GWR freight trilogy in April with the release of the bulky Collett '72XX' 2-8-2T and '5205' 2-8-0T locomotives. The rugged beauty of the '72XX' was captured well, and our review model of 7229 in BR black ran as good as it looked. The '5205' in Great Western green livery featured conical buffer shanks, outside steam pipes and rivet pattern detail differences on the smokebox..

Also in 'OO' gauge, Dapol delighted us with a disc headcode fitted version of its

Class 22. Performance was exemplary, our review model of D6316 in BR green proving smooth and quiet with plenty of power. For something a bit different, Ireland's Murphy Models released its model of the General Motors 071 Co-Co diesel electric locomotive for 'OO' gauge.

In 'N' gauge, April saw Britain's newest freight locomotive added to the Graham Farish roster, when the General Electric Class 70 was released. The bodyshell captured the challenging appearance of the real thing and featured plenty of standout detail.

The eagerly awaited 'N' gauge BR Mk 2a coaching stock arrived in the shape of the First Corridor (FK). Bachmann did a superb job of recreating the correct profile and even the tumblehome and end profile looked spot on. In addition, the Mk 1 horsebox was also added to the 'N' gauge range when we received a sample of the Southern Region version as S96359.

Hornby's BR '8P' 4-6-2 71000 *'Duke of Gloucester'* made the news pages when a decorated sample of the model appeared. Bachmann released decorated sample images of its forthcoming 'OO' gauge Polybulk bogie grain hopper and pre-production shots of its GWR shunter's truck.

May 2013

Dapol's 'N' gauge NBL Class 22 diesel locomotive arrived for review. There were great expectations for this model, given the high quality of the 'OO' gauge version. We needn't have worried, as it proved to be a mini marvel.

Also in 'N' gauge, 'Grampus' departmental wagons arrived. These 'N' gauge models proved highly detailed and contained a removable ballast load allowing them to form a long engineers train with variety. Versions in BR black, BR Indian red, Taunton Concrete Works green and BR engineers 'Dutch' were released.

Big announcements in May saw the now defunct Modelzone commission exclusive 'OO' gauge BR Mk 1 four-wheel CCTs and Mk 1 TPO Brake Stowage vans for release in 2014 from Bachmann. The Keighley and Worth Valley Railway unveiled its latest limited editions – two Bachmann '3F' 0-6-0s - while Hornby showed off its new Railroad Mk 1 carriages with pre-production images of the range in BR maroon. We also caught an enticing first glimpse of the Graham Farish 'N' gauge 'Jinty'. The Midland '1F' and BR Class 101 DMU in 'OO' gauge also appeared with images of the first engineering samples being revealed.

June 2013

June was a comparatively quiet month after a busy start. The highlight was Bachmann reissuing its War Department 'Austerity' 2-8-0 with an upgraded chassis incorporating a 21-pin DCC decoder socket and breathing new life into this model. Our review sample of 90448 in BR black was factory fitted with a DCC decoder on board and operated faultlessly straight from the box.

Bachmann also released its long-awaited 'OO' gauge BR Mk 1 sleeper carriages. Available in BR maroon and BR blue and grey in First (SLF) and Second Class (SLSTP) versions, they allow a new range of train formations to be reproduced.

Hornby's new 'OO' gauge GWR shunter's trucks were also released. Four versions of these four-wheeled wagons arrived for review – two in GWR livery and two in BR livery – labelled for Reading Central, Park Royal, Acton and Gloucester.

July 2013

Occasionally a model arrives in the *Hornby Magazine* office and conversation stops. When the Golden Age Models 'O' gauge 'Merchant Navy' locomotives arrived, that's exactly what happened! These models are superb, featuring opening smokebox doors with full detail inside, sprung axleboxes, all-wheel pick up, etched brass nameplates, oven baked paint finish and Faulhaber motor. Our samples were of air-smoothed 35003 *Royal Mail* in BR lined blue and rebuilt 35004 *Cunard White Star* in BR lined green. Weighing in at just over 3kg each they ran beautifully, and so they should at £2,540 each!

A new 'N' gauge model of the Ivatt '2MT' from Graham Farish arrived eventually, having been announced back in 2007. However, it was worth the wait – our review model of 46440 in BR lined black features Bachmann's new coreless motor for 'N' gauge and it ran silently and smoothly.

The National Railway Museum confirmed a new production run of its highly popular *Deltic* in the BR service livery it carried while in traffic on the Eastern Region of BR.

At its annual open day Bachmann revealed that it is to release five new DCC sound-fitted locomotives featuring

Above: Hornby's GWR shunters truck for 'OO' gauge.

Below: Heljan's abilities to produce small production runs of unusual classes reaped rewards in the 'OO' gauge NBL Class 16.

Golden Age Models 'OO' gauge 'Coronation' carriages and 'Beavertail' observation car.

a new 'economy' sound package produced by Soundtraxx as well as showcasing the latest pre-production samples of its 'J11' 0-6-0, LYR 2-4-2T, Midland '4F' 0-6-0, Class 101 DMUs and decorated samples of LMS 10000 and 10001 in BR green. Hornby confirmed more production delays to around 20 locomotives. *Hornby Magazine* approved its 'OO' gauge ready-to-run diesel brake tender for the start of metal cutting.

August 2013

Heljan continues to produce the unusual, and its 'OO' gauge model of the North British Locomotive Company Type 1, the Class 16 diesel locomotive, arrived for review in August. Two versions were received for review, D8404 in BR green with Stratford yellow warning panels and D8407 in BR green with full yellow ends. Six versions, each limited to 750 models, were produced in total.

Dapol's first version of its 'N' gauge Class 52 'Western' arrived with much excitement in the office. Would it live up to the standards set by the 'OO' version earlier in the year? Well, yes – it did. It's clear that much of the earlier research

has benefitted this model. The centrally mounted motor on our review sample of Osborn Models' limited edition D1000 *Western Enterprise* was virtually silent too – unlike the real thing!

Bachmann's 'OO' gauge Fowler '4F' 0-6-0 caught our eye too. Turned out in BR black offset by red bufferbeams, our review sample of 43924 was beautifully finished and ran like a dream. Staying with Bachmann, it released its all-new LNER 'J39' in 'N' gauge, a good choice of locomotive given its wide area of operation and long career. Featuring a tender drive motor it's clear that Bachmann has done its research and managed to capture the chunky proportions of the Gresley design well.

In the news, Bachmann announced during a press and trade event at the Bluebell Railway that it was to produce a ready-to-run 'OO' gauge model of the 'Brighton Atlantic' 4-4-2. Planned for release in 2015. Two versions will initially appear as 2426 *St Albans Head* in Southern Railway olive green and 32424 *Beachy Head* in BR lined black with early crests.

Bachmann also revealed the first shots

of its new 'OO' gauge GWR '64XX' 0-6-0PT and Tower Models showed pre-production images of its forthcoming two limited edition 'O' gauge Class 52 'Western' locomotives D1000 *Western Enterprise* in desert sand and D1015 *Western Champion* in golden ochre liveries. Other retailer announcements included newcomer Invicta Model Rail announcing it was to produce all the limited edition commissions previously announced by failed retail chain Modelzone and Kernow Model Centre confirming plans for a 'OO' gauge roundhouse inspired inevitably by buildings in Cornwall.

September 2013

As we venture into the modelling season once more, a number of big releases appeared during September including the much-anticipated 'LMS Twins' 10000 and 10001. These large beasts from Bachmann captured the solid look of the prototypes well. Three general release BR Brunswick green versions were made available for review along with a selection of LMS/BR black limited edition versions exclusive to Rails of Sheffield.

Bachmann's Midland Compound 4-4-0 offered a stunning new choice of passenger motive power in 'OO'.

Another milestone model is that of the Class 144 two-car DMU produced by Realtrack Models. This is the first powered model produced by the company and it clearly aimed high. It featured superb detail throughout, right down to intricacies such as the distinctive door and seat grab handles and even the fire extinguisher behind the driver's seat.

On the rolling stock front, Golden Age Models showcased its 'OO' gauge 'Coronation' coaches. These beautifully engineered and crafted vehicles quite simply took our breath away. Available in LNER two-tone blue and BR crimson and cream these articulated sets and their 'beavertail' observation cars are truly sublime.

Making the news, Hornby showed us its latest sample of the 'OO' gauge Gresley 'P2' 2-8-2 *Cock O' The North* in LNER green, due out after Christmas, which looked stunning, and Bachmann revealed the first sample images of its forthcoming 'N' gauge LMS '4F' from the Graham Farish range. Hattons' also revealed decorated samples of its upcoming and much-anticipated exclusive 'OO' gauge Beyer Garratt 2-6-0+0-6-2 locomotives, produced on its behalf by Heljan. Capturing the

complexities of these locomotive giants well, the samples formed the weathering templates for the manufacturer to replicate.

A new manufacturer entered the model railway market in September. DJ Models is owned and operated by Dave Jones who previously had a product development role at Dapol. Dave announced ambitious plans to produce models in 'N' to 'O' gauge over the next few years. Some of those new models include the 'J94' Austerity 0-6-0ST for 'N', 'OO' and 'O' gauge, a Class 23 'Baby Deltic' diesel for 'N' and 'O' gauge and a Class 17 diesel for 'N' gauge. Development work is already at an advanced stage with CAD/CAM drawings underway for each model.

Opinion

Despite the economic climate and some of the production difficulties affecting manufacture over the past 12 months it's clear that the hobby is alive and well with some truly stunning models released.

Our own highlights from the past year in the *Hornby Magazine* office include Bachmann's 'OO' gauge Wainwright 'C', Hornby's 2-BIL EMU and Thompson 'O1' 2-8-0, Dapol's Class 52 and Kernow

Model Railway Centre's Class 205.

In 'N' gauge, our favourites included the six-car Midland Blue Pullman from Graham Farish and Dapol's Class 22 diesel whilst in 'O' gauge it was perhaps inevitably the 'Merchant Navy' steam locomotives from Golden Age Models that impressed the most.

The pace of development never ceases to amaze us with an ever increasing and more diverse range of locomotives and rolling stock being introduced. There is so much in store for the coming months from the characterful Aspinall 2-4-2T from Bachmann to the unique BR '8P' 71000 Duke of Gloucester from Hornby and everything in between that there is bound to be something to suit every taste. Plus we can't forget the burgeoning commission market where Cornish based retailer Kernow Model Rail Centre is leading the way and expecting to release is Adams 'O2' 0-4-4T in 2014 while continuing work on its 'OO' gauge production of the original NBL D600 'Warship' and 'O' gauge Beattie '0298' 2-4-0WT.

Perhaps one of the greatest success stories in waiting is the rise of interest in 'O' gauge. The recent photographs of Heljan's AC Cars railbus, which was shown at the Gauge O Guild exhibition in Telford, could be the catalyst for a raft of new layouts, particularly with the potential of Dapol's Class 08 diesel shunter which is scheduled for release in 2014.

'N' gauge meanwhile is continuing to flourish with Bachmann and Dapol pushing the boundaries and extending the potential of 'N' as a true modellers scale. Products such as the Ivatt '2MT' 2-6-0 really showed what can be done in this scale.

With so many more models still in the pipeline from manufacturers and retailers the next 12 months looks to be just as exciting and you can be assured we'll be bringing you all the latest on those releases each month in *Hornby Magazine*. Watch this space…

Murphy Models Irish 071 Co-Co for 'OO'.

HEAVY FREIGHT
2-8-0s

From the early 1900s to 1968 2-8-0 freight locomotives were amongst the most powerful and profitable locomotives on the railway, hauling huge trains of daily necessities to all parts of the country. **Evan Green-Hughes** looks at the development of these engines and finds out where they can still be seen today.

'WD' 2-8-0 90000 climbs towards Great Ponton on the East Coast Main Line with an up class 'F' goods on May 2 1953. These powerful 2-8-0s were only intended to have a short life, but those operated by BR after the Second World War lasted into the 1960s. Gordon Hepburn/ Rail Archive Stephenson.

Britain of the early 20th century was very different to now. Although there was an extensive network of good roads anything carried over them had to be pulled by horses or traction engines and when any distance was involved this took a long time. Traction engines were heavy and slow, and of course horses could only pull a limited amount of goods, particularly where gradients were involved.

Inevitably most of the country's freight traffic went either by railway or canal with tonnages increasing year upon year as towns and cities became larger and manufacturing expanded, both leading to an almost unquenchable thirst for raw materials and fuel.

Railways had coped well with this demand right from the earliest days of the Stockton and Darlington and locomotive designers had supplied workmanlike and powerful engines, mostly of the 0-6-0 wheel arrangement, to work the trains. However by the turn of the 20th century traffic was increasing so much that in many places lines were being run at full capacity and the only way to expand was to make trains longer.

Solving this apparently simple issue was not quite as easy as it seemed. British freight trains were largely made up of four-wheel wagons without continuous brakes which relied on the weight of the locomotive at the front and brake van at the rear to be able to slow down and eventually stop the train. This same weight was also used to provide sufficient adhesion to get the train on the move. Longer trains needed more power which in turn meant a bigger and more powerful engine but many of the 0-6-0s were already pushing traction, axleload and stability limits.

Bigger locomotives

The answer was to mount the larger locomotive on more axles and a number of companies began to introduce 0-8-0 types with the most numerous fleet built by the London and North Western Railway (LNWR) which introduced to service 282 locomotives between 1892 and 1904. The Great Northern Railway also went with this configuration and built 55 of its 'Q1' class 'Long Toms' starting in 1901 to haul 50 wagon coal trains between Peterborough and London. Engines of this type were very successful but they tended to 'hunt', a railway term describing movement from side to side at the front due to the action of the cylinders. There were also problems in accommodating suitably large cylinders without incurring too much unsupported overhang at the front of the engine – problems which affected a number of designs including passenger 2-2-2s of the late 19th century.

These problems had surfaced simiarly in other parts of the world, particularly

**Above: Robinson GCR
'O4' 2-8-0 63707 passes
Thirstone signalbox on
the climb from Penistone
to Dunford Bridge, on
the notorious Woodhead
route, with a Westbound
coal train in 1952.**
Kenneth Field/Rail Archive
Stephenson.

**Right: The Somerset
and Dorset was the
first component of the
Midland Railway to break
away from the small
engine policy when a
fleet of 11 2-8-0s were
introduced in 1914.
Now in BR ownership
Midland '7F' 2-8-0 53803
crosses the viaduct
near Evercreech with a
Northbound goods on
June 17 1960.**
David Hepburne-Scott/Rail
Archive Stephenson.

in America, where train lengths and therefore weights had grown much earlier than they had in Europe, compounded by poorer quality track than the norm on this side of the Atlantic. There a two-wheel pony truck had been added to the front of an 0-8-0 as early as 1866 and the 2-8-0 had become the standard American freight engine for most of the latter part of the 19th century.

Locomotives of this wheel arrangement had also been built in the UK by private contractors for railways in Australia before the turn of the century but it was the revolutionary Chief Mechanical Engineer of the Great Western Railway (GWR), George Jackson Churchward - an advocate of American practice - who was first to adopt this design for use in the UK itself.

The GWR was moving massive amounts of freight and minerals, particularly from the coalfields of South Wales towards London and needed a much larger freight engine. Churchward knew that if he used the boiler he'd recently designed for his 4-6-0s with the same outside cylinders he would have a machine of outstanding qualities for freight if he adopted the 2-8-0 wheel arrangement. The resulting prototype, 97, appeared in 1903 and underwent

a two-year trial period during which it was realised that more power could be obtained if the cylinder diameter was increased and the boiler pressure raised from 200psi to 225psi.

Development of the boiler for both 4-6-0 and 2-8-0 designs led to Swindon's famous Standard No. 1 boiler, which served with distinction for the next 60-odd years. No 97 was soon renumbered 2800 and was followed by 166 broadly similar locomotives which were so well designed, economical to operate and popular with the crews that

active consideration was being given to building more of them even after the nationalisation of British Railways some 45 years later.

The following year another 2-8-0 was introduced to service, this time by the LNWR where George Whale began a programme to rebuild some of the 'B4' four-cylinder compound 0-8-0s, which had always suffered from problems arising from excessive front overhang. The rebuilt locomotives, which became the Class 'E' 2-8-0, were not as successful as the GWR design as they were not a completely new design, but 25 more were converted between 1904 and 1908, with two of these further improved in 1907/1908 by being fitted with larger boilers. The 24 remaining engines were eventually rebuilt as two-cylinder simple 0-8-0s and incorporated in the 'G1' class.

Inspiration to others

The continued success of the Churchward '28XX' class pointed the way for other designers and one-by-one others were to copy the concept of the 2-8-0 with large boiler, two outside cylinders and simple layout.

In 1911 John Robinson of the Great Central Railway designed a locomotive which ultimately exceeded, in numerical terms at least, the GWR design when he came up with his Class '8K', later to become known as the LNER 'O4'.

This was essentially a superheated version of an earlier 0-8-0 with the front end supported on a pony truck and was designed in anticipation of an increase in long-distance traffic arising from the opening of the company's new docks

MAJOR 2-8-0 CLASSES IN THE UK

Class	Year	Company	Boiler	Wheels	Weight	Power
'28XX'	1903	GWR	Taper	4ft 7 ½in	75tons 10cwt	35,380lbs
'8K' ('O4')	1911	GCR	Parallel	4ft 8 ½in	72tons 10cwt	31,325lbs
'O1'	1913	GNR	Parallel	4ft 8in	76tons 4cwt	33,736lbs
'7F'	1914	S&D	Parallel	4ft 7 ½in	64tons 15cwt	35,295lbs
'8F'	1935	LMS	Taper	4ft 8 ½in	72tons 10cwt	32,440lbs
'WD'	1943	War Dept	Parallel	4ft 8 ½in	70tons 5cwt	34,215lbs
'S160'	1942	USA	Parallel	4ft 9in	72tons 10cwt	31,490lbs

at Immingham. These free-steaming (though not according to GWR firemen) and steady riding engines were an immediate success and within three years 126 had been constructed not only by the Great Central itself but by private builders Kitson and Co and North British on their behalf.

When the Great War broke out in 1914 the Ministry of Munitions through its Railway Operating Division took up the design as a wartime standard and consequently 521 further '8Ks' were built for service both at home and overseas. These locomotives acquitted themselves well in all corners of Europe, further underlining the suitability of the

2-8-0 for heavy freight work. Once hostilities were at an end examples were quickly snapped up by the LNWR and the GWR with more examples being bought after the 1923 Grouping by the London Midland and Scottish Railway (LMS) and the London and North Eastern Railway (LNER). As with the GWR 2-8-0s the 'O4s' were very long lived with some lasting into the 1960s.

Two years after the GCR's 'O4' first hit the rails the Great Northern Railway produced its own 2-8-0, with design work being done by the then young Nigel Gresley, for use on heavy coal traffic between Peterborough and London and to augment and replace the

Gresley introduced a class of three-cylinder 2-8-0s for the LNER in the 'O2' 2-8-0. 'O2' 3482 heads North from Hatfield with goods train for New England on March 31 1938. Collin Turner/Rail Archive Stephenson.

Right: Oil-fired GWR '28XX' 2-8-0 4808 (ex-2834) passes Norton Fitzwarren with a down goods in May 1948 as it puts on an impressive display. E Griffith/Rail Archive Stephenson.

Far right: The GWR was the instigator of the 2-8-0 freight engine in British locomotive design with locomotive 97 in 1903. It led onto the '28XX' class and later Collett developed the design further to create the '2884' class which featured a side window cab and other improvements. GWR '2884' 2-8-0 3861 approaches West Rusilip with an up freight in November 1951. Lewis Coles/ Rail Archive Stephenson.

'Long Toms'. The 'O1' 2-8-0 (later to become LNER 'O3') was an attractive locomotive with raised running plate above the driving wheels which did away with the need for splashers and which gave the engine a much more modern appearance.

A 5ft 6in diameter superheated boiler fed two 21in diameter cylinders which produced a tractive effort of 33,736lbs. Particular attention was paid to the design of the front pony truck which was of a double bolster swing link design which assisted the engine by guiding it when negotiating crossovers. I
n service they proved capable of hauling 80 loaded wagons, around 20 more than the earlier 0-8-0s, but bulk introduction of the class was interrupted by the outbreak of the First World War, by which time only five had been built.

A further 15 were eventually constructed in 1918 and 1919. A three-cylinder version, the 'O2', followed in 1918 which brought the tractive effort up to 36,470lbs and which ran to several variants, including some with different boilers, although all had side-window cabs.

Midland developments

Although the Midland Railway had its own heavy traffic up to London from coalfields and manufacturing centres in its area it did not follow the lead of the other companies and instead stuck with smaller locomotives, particularly the 0-6-0s, for hauling its freight trains. It was, however, also responsible for providing motive power for the Somerset and Dorset Railway (S&D) which it jointly owned with the London and South Western Railway (LSWR).

There the main line climbed to 811ft above sea level and contained many single line sections which meant that a powerful goods locomotive with a good turn of speed was required. The Midland Railway agreed that something which differed from its usual policy was called for and the job was given to the Chief Draughtsman James Clayton who designed a simple and powerful engine based round the parallel boiler previously used on the company's compound passenger locomotives. This 2-8-0 was always distinguishable as the large outside cylinders were inclined so as to give sufficient clearance for

platforms and 11 were eventually built between 1914 and 1925. They remained on their home territory for all of their lives with the last not being withdrawn until 1964.

With numerous examples of the GCR and GWR designs available there was little progress with the development of the 2-8-0 in the years immediately after the First World War, although there were numerous detail improvements, with the Western engines being redesigned by Collett to accommodate a larger side window cab and with some of the Great Central's '8Ks' being fitted with larger boilers.

However, the LMS was still struggling with the legacy of the Midland Railway's 'small engine' policy and by 1930 the situation in the operating department had reached crisis point as many of the company's locomotives were by then

READY-TO-RUN 2-8-0S, 'OO' AND 'N' GAUGE

Class	Company	Scale	Manufacturer	Availability
'28XX' 2-8-0	GWR	'OO'	www.hornby.com	Current
'2884' 2-8-0	GWR	'OO'	www.hornby.com	Current
'2884' 2-8-0	GWR	'N'	www.dapol.co.uk	Current
'O4' 2-8-0	GCR/LNER	'OO'	www.bachmann.co.uk	Current
'O1' 2-8-0	LNER	'OO'	www.hornby.com	Current
'O2' 2-8-0	LNER	'OO'	www.heljan.dk	Due 2014
'7F' 2-8-0	S&D	'OO'	www.bachmann.co.uk	Current
'8F' 2-8-0	LMS	'OO'	www.hornby.com	Current
'8F' 2-8-0	LMS	'N'	www.bachmann.co.uk	Current
'WD' 2-8-0	WD	'OO'	www.bachmann.co.uk	Current
'WD' 2-8-0	WD	'N'	www.bachmann.co.uk	Current

Left: While the Robinson 'O4' was a capable locomotive, Thompson undertook rebuilding of part of the class to use standard components and forming the 'O1' class. On June 7 1958 'O1' 2-8-0 63676 leaves Sherwood Rise tunnel with a short down goods on the Great Central Main Line. John Wilson/Rail Archive Stephenson.

far too small for the traffic which was being worked and consequently there was a great deal of uneconomic double heading.

In 1931 the LMS Board of Directors headhunted William Stanier who was then Works Manager at Swindon, as the new Chief Mechanical Engineer he brought with him many Great Western ideas including the concept

The War years

By virtue of its modernity and success, the '8F' design was also selected for bulk production by the Government and another 208 were ordered by the War Department (WD) from Beyer, Peacock and Co and the North British Locomotive Company with the Railway Executive Committee ordering a further 245 on behalf of the LMS in 1943-1944.

a further three from the Longmoor Military Railway in 1957 meaning that 666 examples were in service until withdrawals began in 1960 and an incredible 150 were to last until the final year of steam on BR, a fine testament to a rugged and reliable design.

A budget 2-8-0

Although the Stanier '8F' was eminently suitable for its wartime duties there was a massive shortage of raw materials for locomotive construction and consequently designer Robert Riddles was commissioned to come up with a version which was cheaper to produce. These machines were expected to have a short working life and could accordingly be built to a lower specification.

The resulting engine, the War Department ('WD') 2-8-0, was closely based on the '8F' but used a cheaper parallel boiler and had a firebox made of steel rather than of the more expensive copper. Production changes decreased the time it took to build each locomotive with the result that from 1943 onwards production for the War Department swapped from building '8Fs' to the new more economical type.

> *"The War Department 2-8-0 was closely based on the Stanier '8F', but used a cheaper parallel boiler and had a firebox made of steel rather than copper to save money. A total of 935 were built between 1943 and 1945."*

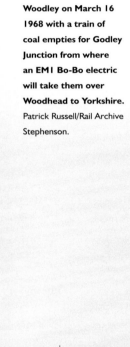

Below: Stanier LMS '8F' 2-8-0 48374 approaches Woodley on March 16 1968 with a train of coal empties for Godley Junction from where an EM1 Bo-Bo electric will take them over Woodhead to Yorkshire.
Patrick Russell/Rail Archive Stephenson.

of standardisation, the use of the taper boiler and the suitability of the 2-8-0 as a heavy duty freight engine.

Within a few years of his appointment he had reversed the 'small engine' policy and had designed a fleet of powerful locomotives able to easily carry out the tasks required of them. One of these was a two-cylinder 2-8-0 which shared many design features with his existing mixed traffic 'Black Five' 4-6-0 and proved to be an outstanding success – the last being withdrawn in 1968. Within a few years of their introduction in 1935 the new '8Fs', as they became known, had revolutionised heavy freight services throughout the LMS region and consigned many older designs to the scrapyard. 137 were built at Crewe works and 69 more by the Vulcan Foundry before the Second World War broke out and a further 125 were constructed during the hostilities as traffic increased.

These were built by the GWR, the LNER and the Southern Railway while the final 68 locomotives went to the LNER which constructed 43 of them itself and received the final 25 from the Southern's Brighton works.

Those built for the War Department were exported to assist with the war effort and saw service in countries such as Iran, Italy, Egypt, Palestine and Turkey where many remained at the end of hostilities. Some had extremely long service careers abroad, particularly those which had found their way to Turkey, some of which were still in service until the early 1980s and known as 'Churchills' as a result. Some were sunk on their way to action and the ghostly remains can still be seen by keen divers in the Red Sea.

Of the 852 locomotives built to this design 624 passed into British Railways ownership and the newly-nationalised railway bought another 39 from ex War Department stock in 1948 and added

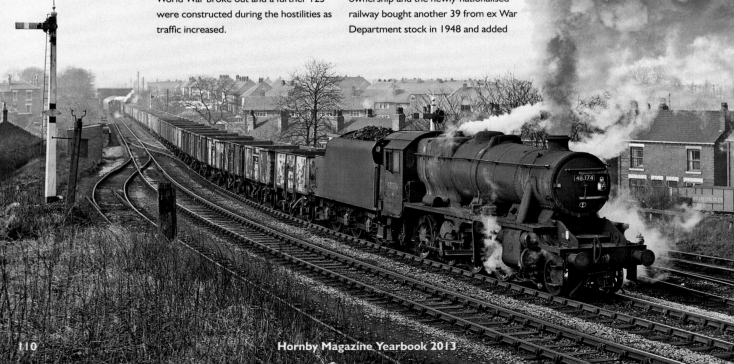

A total of 935 were built in anticipation of the retaking of Europe and almost all of them were ferried across the Channel following D Day in June 1945. Most returned after the conflict was over and 733 were taken into stock by British Railways. Of the others 184 remained in mainland Europe, particularly in Holland, and 12 ended up in Hong Kong. Many of the UK examples were in traffic almost until the final days of steam, far beyond their anticipated life expectancy, and they proved to be reliable and strong locomotives, although with a reputation for rough riding.

Despite the production of so many of the 'WD' 2-8-0s the Government knew that more heavy freight machines would be required as the war progressed and consequently they turned to the Americans who were able to supply their wartime equivalent of the 'WD' design, the 'S160'. These had been designed for very easy construction and contained a number of compromises to achieve this and consequently were to prove not as reliable as the Riddles equivalent, though they were extremely powerful and easy to maintain – better in the latter respect than the British designs.

800 locomotives to this design were constructed by Alco, Baldwin and Lima Locomotive Works and were shipped to South Wales in 1942/1943 where they were commissioned ready for use when the invasion came. Of these 400 saw service within the British Isles where they were used to haul supply trains in advance of the invasion or to stand in for damaged stock. Just before D Day all the locomotives were gathered together and prepared for service by American personnel based in South Wales. None returned to the UK again prior to the preservation era. Around 2,000 of these machines were built in total and they saw service all over Europe, as well as in Africa, Asia and South America.

End of the line

Following the creation of British Railways in 1948 no further locomotives to the 2-8-0 wheel arrangement were built and instead when the new standard freight locomotives were designed they were to the longer 2-10-0 wheel arrangement in the form of the brilliant and peerless '9Fs'. Although these new locomotives were more powerful and better than almost any other freight locomotives ever built, with the writing on the wall for steam traction from the 1950s

onwards there were never going to be enough of them to replace the older 0-8-0 types, never mind the still effective 2-8-0s from the GWR, LMS and LNER. This meant that many of the 2-8-0s lasted until the end of steam on their respective regions.

Happily this meant that several were to pass into the hands of preservationists and as a result some have been restored and can be seen at work on some of our heritage railways. Stanier '8F' 48151 has been registered for main line operation and can still be seen working excursions and passenger trains on the network.

Of the larger classes there are 15 of the Great Western's '28XXs' and their descendants still in existence. Of these five can be seen in action with 2807 at the Gloucestershire Warwickshire Railway, 2857 at the Severn Valley Railway, 3802 at the Llangollen Railway, 3803 at the Battlefield Railway and 3850 which is usually at the West Somerset Railway. Others have previously steamed and are currently in store and 2818 is on display at the National Railway Museum.

Only one of Robinson's '8Ks' - or 'O4' if you prefer - has survived in this country, despite the large number built, and 1912-built 63601 is based at the Great Central Railway. Two more are preserved in Australia. The former Somerset and Dorset 2-8-0s have done much better despite the small number constructed, and there are two available for the public to see, 53808 can be found at the West Somerset Railway while 53809 is currently undergoing rebuild at the Midland Railway - Butterley after recent service at the North Yorkshire Moors Railway.

As may be expected some of the large number of Stanier '8Fs' have survived, with seven former main line examples making it into preservation. As

mentioned above 48151 is on the main line while 48624 is at the Great Central Railway. 48773, after a career in the UK, Iran and Suez before returning to the UK in 1955, is displayed at the Severn Valley, though it is currently out of use, and 48431 is similarly on show at Oxenhope on the Keighley and Worth Valley Railway. Of the others 48305 is under major overhaul at the Great Central Railway while 48173 is still in scrapyard condition. 48518 has been dismantled to provide parts for other projects.

Two other '8Fs' have been re-imported from overseas, one of which, as LMS 8476, runs at the Gloucestershire Warwickshire Railway and the other is currently being rebuilt at the North Norfolk.

Surprisingly none of the BR owned 'WD' 2-8-0s survived into preservation, being cut up as soon as they were withdrawn, but a similar locomotive which had been exported to Sweden was repatriated by the Keighley and Worth Valley Railway where it was restored and it runs today as 90733. Eight 'S160s' have been returned to the country at various times of which Churnet Valley Railway based 5197 is in steam (though working at the North Yorkshire Moors Railway during late 2013) and others are under overhaul.

For more than 50 years the 2-8-0 dominated the heavy haulage of freight in the UK and made an immeasurable contribution to the economy of the country. The type also did more than its fair share of work in the global conflicts of the era. Fortunately with so many examples preserved we will always be reminded of the good work that they did and hopefully be able to see them continue in service on our heritage railways and the main line for many more years to come.

Above: One of the most distinctive 2-8-0 designs to run on British railways was the American built 'S160' 2-8-0. Brought to Britain as part of the War effort in the 1940s, they were used to haul supply trains. USATC 2-8-0 2088 stands at an unknown LMS shed in the 1940s.
Rail Archive Stephenson.

Twelve Trees Junction
ROLLING STOCK AND OPERATION

Building a scenic model railway is one thing, but making it work with accurate train formations is what makes it realistic. **Mike Wild** describes the formations and explains how Twelve Trees Junction will work.

Right: BR 'Standard Four' 4-6-0 75072 coasts through Twelve Trees Junction with a Southbound parcels working as a 2-EPB departs heading North.

Below: BR 'Standard Four' 2-6-0 76053 heads North with a mixed goods and passes the carriage sheds at Twelve Trees Junction. In the distance a 4-CEP is slowing for the stop at the station.

Stocking a main line layout is a tremendous challenge. It needs a large collection of locomotives, carriages and wagons. Twelve Trees Junction fits into the large layout category and in fact it is the largest layout we've ever built for *Hornby Magazine* or our yearbooks.

In the past our largest layout measured 16ft x 9ft, including the fiddle yard, but Twelve Trees will fill an impressive 32ft

x 8ft once it is fully assembled with its fiddle yards. That means it will need a large amount of rolling stock too!

Fortunately the collection of Southern Region stock acquired for Bay Street Shed means we already have a head start with some 50 locomotives, more than 60 carriages and a healthy collection of multiple units. Plus we also have an extensive fleet of BR steam era goods wagons which have been amassed for

operation with all of the magazine's layouts including Bolsover and Seven Lane Pit, Topley Dale (Yearbook No. 5) and St Stephens Road (Yearbook No. 4). However, there is always room for more and the growing range of ready-to-run products across the board.

The variety of trains to be operated on Twelve Trees covers all three sections of the Southern – the Eastern, Central and Western. Our aim though isn't to stick

rigidly to one of these as we wish to run as wide a range of train formations as possible on the layout.

The locomotive fleet

The steam fleet for Twelve Trees is heavily populated with Bulleid 'Pacifics' and BR Standards. The fleet consists of five air-smoothed 'Light Pacifics', four rebuilt 'West Country' 4-6-2s, three 'Merchant Navy' 4-6-2s plus a trio of 'Q1' 0-6-0s, a BR 'Standard Five' 4-6-0, two 'Standard Four' 4-6-0s, a 'Standard Four' 2-6-0 and more.

However, earlier designs are prominent too with the likes of a Wainwright 'C' class 0-6-0, a Drummond '700' 0-6-0, 'M7' 0-4-4Ts, and 'T9' 4-4-0 also forming part of the roster. Naturally Maunsell's 'King Arthur' 4-6-0s, 'Schools' 4-4-0s and 'N' 2-6-0s are all part of the fleet.

The Southern Region steam fleet has seen little action over the past two years since no layout has been available to operate them on and one of the processes which will occur before Twelve Trees Junction's debut

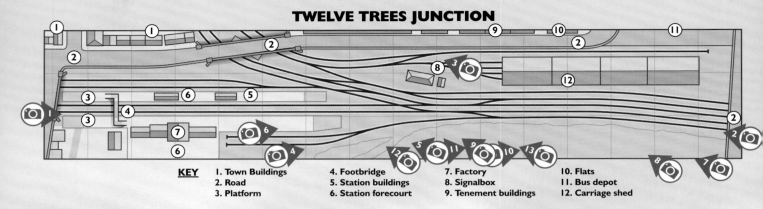

TWELVE TREES JUNCTION

is upgrading of weathering to meet our current standards. Other important jobs will include oiling of mechanisms and, where necessary, DCC fitting. The plan is to equip a substantial part of the fleet with DCC sound over time. Already thanks to the conversion of St Stephens Road to DCC there are 12 sound fitted locomotives available including a pair of 'West Countrys', two Maunsell 'N' 2-6-0s, a Drummond 'M7' 0-4-4T and 'T9' 4-4-0 and a handful of BR Standards. While Southern motive power will lead the locomotive fleet we will also include a handful of other locomotives too for use on London transfer freights. These will include 'WD' and '8F' 2-8-0s together with BR '9F' 2-10-0s amongst

3 A pair of 2-BIL EMUs move slowly back into the carriage sidings after cleaning.

Left: 2-H DEMU
1108 rumbles
into Twelve Trees bay
platform as a cement train
heads North lead by a pair
of BRCW Type 3s.

Below: A Bulleid
'Q1' 0-6-0 passes
through Twelve Trees with
a breakdown train. On the
left a 2-H DEMU ticks over
in the bay platform.

others.

On the diesel front the inclusion
of transfer freights opens up a world
of opportunities when it comes to
locomotive classes. Normally it is only
the BRCW Class 33s associated with the
Southern Region alongside the electro-
diesel Class 73s. However, through the
transfer freights Twelve Trees diesel fleet
will include classes 15, 16, 20, 24, 25,
27, 31 and 37. Plus we will also have the
opportunity to run Class 42 'Warships'
on Waterloo-Exeter workings and Class
47s on Pullman and inter-regional trains.

When operating the layout in the mid
1950s we also have the opportunity to
run Southern Region prototype diesel

10203, built from a Silver Fox kit, and
also London Midland & Scottish Railway
prototype 10001 in BR black livery.
These will add more variety to the
roster, but are most suited to the earliest
period we will run Twelve Trees in
covering 1953-1955.

Multiple units

We have a healthy collection of Electric
Multiple Units (EMUs) for Twelve Trees

too covering ready-to-run and kit built
units and it is planned that this fleet will
expand in the future too.

One of the most common units in
the fleet is the 4-CEP four-car unit
from Bachmann with four available to
the layout. In addition we have a MLV,
again by Bachmann, which will operate
with a pair of 4-CEPs to form a boat
train formation. We plan to add a 4-BEP
buffet unit to the fleet in the future too
through modifications to a 4-CEP.

Other BR built units in the fleet
include the BR 2-EPB and a kit
built model of the Bulleid
designed 2-EPB and the
BR 4-EPB. Plus we

 6 Framed by the signal gantry, BR 'Standard Five' 73082 Camelot heads the daily Southbound parcels working through Twelve Trees after being held on the slow line for an express to pass.

7 Bulleid 'West Country' 4-6-2 34007 Wadebridge races North towards London with an express.

8 A pair of BRCW Type 3s head North with a daily cement working while a third Type 3 is held at the signal with a fuel oil train for an express to pass.

also have a pair of 2-H DEMUs from Kernow Model Rail Centre available for the layout.

Earlier period units are the Hornby 5-BEL 'Brighton Belle' unit and the recently released 2-BIL EMU which strengthen the fleet still further. We also have a 4-SUB EMU, but due to current motor bogie problems it is kept in the carriage sidings rather than being a working train.

Rolling stock

The carriage fleet for Twelve Trees Junction is extensive and consists of two rakes of BR Southern Region green Mk 1s plus a carmine and cream rake of Mk 1s to represent the most modern locomotive hauled trains of the period. However, these are bolstered by a rake of Bulleid coaches which are currently being repainted and renumbered for the layout to expand the passenger fleet further.

Representing older passenger stock is an extensive fleet of Maunsell carriages. There are a mixture of two and three cars sets available as well as loose carriages to strengthen sets covering both BR Southern Region green and a lesser used four-car and two-car set in BR carmine and cream. The final addition to the Maunsell fleet is a push-pull set for operation with an 'M7' 0-4-4T from the bay platform.

Parcels and goods stock is drawn mainly from ready-to-run ranges, but with a number of kit built or repainted vehicles included. Formations include a rake of 20ton coal hoppers, mixed goods for transfer freights, van trains, an oil train and a growing collection of wagons to form engineers' trains. These include repainted Hornby 'Trout' hoppers, Heljan 'Dogfish' hoppers, Dapol 'Grampus' and kit built wagons such as a 'Ling' and 'Lamprey' wagons from Chivers Finelines.

Digital control

Twelve Trees Junction has been designed to be a busy layout. The junction in the centre is the focal point of operations and its complex track layout should make it entertaining for both operators and viewers alike.

The sheer size of this layout means that it will only ever be fully assembled at exhibitions. The scenic section is 16ft long and once the two return loop fiddle yards are complete it will need 32ft of floor space and require at least

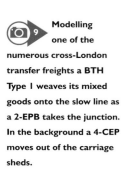
Modelling one of the numerous cross-London transfer freights a BTH Type 1 weaves its mixed goods onto the slow line as a 2-EPB takes the junction. In the background a 4-CEP moves out of the carriage sheds.

With the carriage sheds behind a pair of 2-BIL EMUs approach Twelve Trees Junction.

An unusual visitor to the Southern, BR Sulzer Type 2 D7648 leads a transfer freight back towards the Midland Region's Willesden depot from Norwood Junction.

The junction arrangement allows multiple train movements at Twelve Trees Junction. As a Maunsell 'N' 2-6-0 leads a van train through on the main line a BR '4MT' 2-6-0 slows to take the goods loop in the background.

three operators at any one time. Train formations will be long to represent expresses and, due to the design of the fiddle yards, we'll also be able to have a large selection of trains ready to operate.

Twelve Trees will be operated with digital control. The plan is to use Hornby's RailMaster system and make the best use of its handheld applications which have launched this year. These connect to a 'main' computer using a wireless network which means that additional operators can have full control of locomotives and points through devices such as iPads, iPhones, Android tablets and more.

The plan for Twelve Trees is that one operator will have the main computer and become the signalman for the layout. His role will be to manage the routes of all the trains which pass through Twelve Trees Junction. Beyond this up to four drivers can be employed on the layout – three for the main lines and one for the carriage sidings.

One of the beauties of Twelve Trees trackplan is that it allows complex movements to occur, much like you would experience on the real railway near the capital. These include goods trains approaching the junction from under the skew bridge and entering the goods loop while a stopping train departs from the loop platform and an express thunders through in the opposite direction heading through the station. This is what will make Twelve Trees an enjoyable spectacle.

As well as main line movements there is plenty of scope for additional operation. Along the front of the layout from the bay platform a branch shuttle can run to its own dedicated sidings in the London end fiddle yard – either an 'M7' with a push-pull set or a Class 205 DEMU. Meanwhile at the back of the layout an operator can have full control over the EMU carriage sidings, moving stock in and out of the sheds and dispatching units to the loops for onwards movement either towards London or into the station to form a passenger working. We also intend splitting and joining EMU formations in the station and carriage sidings through the flexibility of DCC.

A dream come true

Twelve Trees Junction is an operator's dream. It offers flexibility, scale length trains, drivable locomotives with sound – and in some cases smoke generators too – and a plentiful supply of trains and different movements to keep the public entertained at exhibitions too.

It has been a thoroughly enjoyable experience building Twelve Trees so far and we're excited to be able to debut it as a fully working scenic layout at the Hornby Magazine Great Electric Train Show in October 2014. There is a lot of work to be done before then including building fiddle yards and developing the scenery and rolling stock further, but it will all be worthwhile.

Keep an eye on the Staff Projects section of *Hornby Magazine* for more on Twelve Trees in the run up to its debut…

 A pair of 4-CEP EMUs thunder through the junction heading North.

Heljan is breaking new ground by working its first solo steam project following work with Hattons on its LMS Garratt. Their first choice is the three-cylinder Gresley 'O2' 2-8-0. On July 9 1949 63958 passes March East Junction with a Temple Mills to Whitemoor goods. Gordon Hepburn/Rail Archive Stephenson.

Forward to 2014

Could it get any better? Well if plans for almost 60 new locomotive models across 'N', 'OO' and 'O' gauge in 2012 weren't enough the total now stands at more than 70 in 2013! **Mike Wild** reveals all...

Each year in late September I sit down and take stock, write out lists and while away an evening pondering over what is coming next. And each year I've been shocked at the sheer volume of new locomotive models which are planned for release in the coming 18 months.

Turn the clock back even 15 years and it was a very different picture. New releases were rarities, not the norm, and in the *Hornby Magazine* office it is now unusual for a month to pass without even one brand new release or upgrade gracing our reviews desk.

This year there are 72 new models in varying stages of production. Some are about to arrive in the shops: in October

we were expecting to see samples of the GWR 'Star' 4-6-0 from Hornby, GWR 'Dukedog' 4-4-0 from Bachmann – both in 'OO' gauge – as well as the 'O' gauge 'Western' from Heljan and, potentially, Graham Farish's new Fairburn 2-6-4T. That's a hefty delivery, but it is just the tip of the iceberg!

'OO' gauge

4mm scale and 'OO' gauge modelling is at the top of its game right now and has historically been the market leader in the UK. Right now there are 30 new locomotive and multiple unit models planned for the scale ranging in size from the diminutive Sentinel 4wDM shunter from Hornby to the giant LMS Beyer

Garratt 2-6-0+0-6-2 from Hatton's of Liverpool.

Excitingly, steam is taking a strong hold in this sector right now with 17 out of the 30 new productions being from this subject line. This is down to the fact that virtually all of the BR main line diesel locomotives have been produced while electric traction, overall at least, still appears to be a niche subject.

As this Yearbook closed for press a number of models were on the verge of release. Bachmann had three on the cards for December/January with its GWR 'Dukedog' 4-4-0, LYR '2P' 2-4-2T and LNER 'J11' 0-6-0 all expected to arrive in a period which also promised the GWR 'Star' 4-6-0 and BR '8P' 4-6-2

'OO' GAUGE NEW RELEASES FOR 2012/2013

Class	Region	Manufacturer	Due
GWR 'Dukedog' 4-4-0	Western	Bachmann	2013
Adams 'O2' 0-4-4T	Southern	Kernow MRC	2014
LYR 2-4-2T	Midland	Bachmann	2013
LMS Garratt 2-6-0+0-6-2	Midland	Hattons	2013
Robinson 'J11' 0-6-0	Eastern	Bachmann	2014
BR '8P' 4-6-2 71000	Midland	Hornby	2013
LNER 'P2' 2-8-2	Eastern	Hornby	2014
GWR 'Hall' 4-6-0	Western	Hornby	2014
GWR 'Star' 4-6-0	Western	Hornby	2013
LMS Stanier 2-6-0	Midland	Bachmann	2014
Midland '1F' 0-6-0T	Midland	Bachmann	2014
GWR '64XX' 0-6-0PT	Western	Bachmann	2014
LBSCR 'H2' 4-4-2	Southern	Bachmann	2015
LBSCR 'E4' 0-6-2T	Southern	Bachmann	2014
LNER 'O2' 2-8-0	Eastern	Heljan	2014
LNER 'J94' 0-6-0ST	Eastern	DJ Models	2014
SR 'USA' 0-6-0T	Southern	Bauer Media	2014
Sentinel 4wDM	Various	Hornby	2013
AEC GWR streamlined railcar	Western	Dapol	TBC
AC Cars railbus	Western	Heljan	2013
Bulleid 10201-10203 1-Co-Co-1	Southern	Kernow MRC	TBC
Class 21/29 Bo-Bo	Scottish	Dapol	2014
Class 23 Bo-Bo (original condition)	Eastern	Heljan	2013
Class 24/1 Bo-Bo	Various	Bachmann	2014
Class 40 1-Co-Co-1 (upgraded tooling)	Midland/ Eastern	Bachmann	2013
Class 41 'Warship' A1A-A1A	Western	Kernow MRC	2014
Class 43 'Warship' B-B	Western	Bachmann	2014
Class 73 Bo-Bo	Southern	Dapol	2014
Class 101 DMU	Various	Bachmann	2013
Class 143 DMU	Various	Realtrack Models	2014

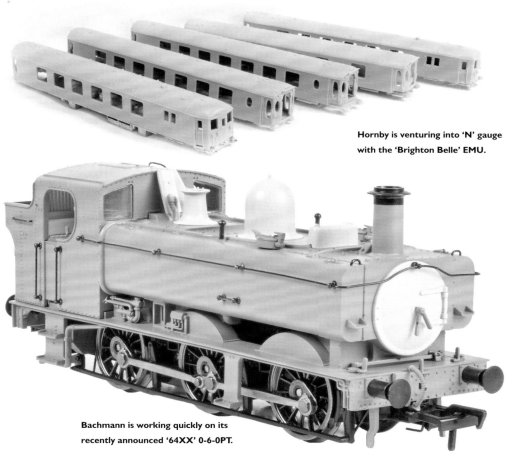

Hornby is venturing into 'N' gauge with the 'Brighton Belle' EMU.

Bachmann is working quickly on its recently announced '64XX' 0-6-0PT.

71000 *Duke of Gloucester* from Hornby.

Elsewhere Hatton's was just a few weeks away from receiving the first production models of its eagerly anticipated Garratt for 'OO' gauge offering the truly tantalising spectacle of these articulated monsters as a ready-to-run model.

Late August and early September were exciting times as two brand new steam models were announced for 'OO'. First Bachmann revealed that it would produce the Billinton 'H2' 4-4-2 for the Southern Railway/Region on August 31 while seven days later DJ Models entered the market as a brand new manufacturer – its first 'OO' model being the Hunslet 'J94' 0-6-0ST.

The diesel and electric market has begun to slow of late, although that isn't reflected in the past few month's big releases. However, in September there were 13 new diesel models planned for 'OO' down one from 2012 when 14 were

Hattons LMS Garratt 2-6-0+0-6-2 is on the home straight and expected to become available in November or December 2013.

'N' GAUGE NEW RELEASES FOR 2012/2013

Class	Region	Manufacturer	Due
GWR '64XX' 0-6-0PT	Western	Bachmann	2014
GWR 'Castle' 4-6-0	Western	Bachmann	2014
GWR 'Grange' 4-6-0	Western	Dapol	2014
Bulleid 'Merchant Navy' 4-6-2	Southern	Bachmann	2014
SR Maunsell 'Schools' 4-4-0	Southern	Dapol	2014
SR Maunsell 'N' 2-6-0	Southern	Bachmann	2014
Bulleid 'West Country' 4-6-2	Southern	Dapol	2014
Bulleid rebuilt 'West Country' 4-6-2	Southern	Dapol	2014
Fowler 'Jinty' 0-6-0T	Midland	Bachmann	2014
Fowler '4F' 0-6-0	Midland	Bachmann	2014
Stanier 'Duchess' 4-6-2	Midland	Bachmann	2013
Peppercorn 'A2' 4-6-2	Eastern	Bachmann	2014
LMS Fairburn 2-6-4T	Midland/Southern	Bachmann	2013
Riddles '4MT' 2-6-4T	Various	Bachmann	2013
LNER 'J94' 0-6-0ST	Eastern	DJ Models	TBC
Class 17 Bo-Bo	Eastern/Scottish	DJ Models	TBC
Class 23 Bo-Bo	Eastern	DJ Models	TBC
Class 25/1 Bo-Bo	Midland/Eastern	Bachmann	2014
Class 27 Bo-Bo	Scottish	Dapol	2013
Class 33 Bo-Bo	Southern	Dapol	2013
Class 31 A1A-A1A	Various	Bachmann	2013
Class 37/4 Co-Co	Various	Bachmann	2014
Class 37/5 Co-Co	Various	Bachmann	2014
Class 47/7 Co-Co	Various	Bachmann	2014
Class 50 Co-Co	Midland/Western	Dapol	2013
Class 55 'Deltic' Co-Co	Eastern	Bachmann	2014
Class 59 Co-Co	Various	Dapol	2013
Class 92 Co-Co	Southern/Midland	Dapol	TBA
Class 142 DMU	Midland/Eastern	Dapol	2013
5-BEL Pullman EMU	Southern	Hornby Arnold N	2014

on the cards.

Some of these are products which had previously been announced including Dapol's Class 21/29 and Class 73 together with Kernow Model Rail Centre's commissions of the NBL D600 'Warships' and Bulleid prototypes 10201-10203. There are new additions though including the Class 24/1 and Class 43 'Warship' from Bachmann while Hornby produced the 2-BIL EMU which never made it into our lists – it was announced in December 2012 and released almost instantly in January 2013!

While the pace of new diesel and electric models has clearly slowed, the subjects in question continue to be just as enthralling. The next new diesel release expected in the *Hornby Magazine* office for 'OO' was the AC Cars railbus closely followed by the original condition

Class 23 'Baby Deltic', both from Heljan. Bachmann's upgraded and improved Class 40 was also expected to arrive in December/January.

'N' gauge

As a scale 'N' gauge continues to flourish and every year an ever more breathtaking range of models is announced to tempt us! This year is no exception and with the recent release of the Ivatt '2MT' 2-6-0 in Bachmann's Graham Farish range and the 'Western' from Dapol there is already much in favour for this scale.

Interestingly diesel and steam models are equal in 'N' gauge with the 30 new models planned being of this nature spilt evenly between the two sectors. The total number of 'N' gauge models in planning and production is also up from

The options for ready-to-run diesel classes are diminishing by the year. Amongst the latest announcements from Bachmann is the NBL built 'Warship' diesel-hydraulic. D860 *Victorious* passes through Sidney Gardens, Bath, with an Up express for Paddington on May 2 1965. Brian Stephenson.

Class	Region	Manufacturer	Due
Beattie '0298' 2-4-0WT	Southern	Kernow MRC	2014
Stroudley 'A1X' 0-6-0T	Southern	Dapol	2014
LNER 'J94' 0-6-0ST	Eastern	DJ Models	TBC
AC Cars railbus	Western	Heljan	2014
Class 08 0-6-0	All	Dapol	2014
Class 23 Bo-Bo	Eastern	DJ Models	TBC
Class 25 Bo-Bo	Midland/Eastern	Heljan	2015
Class 40 1-Co-Co-1	Midland/Eastern	Heljan	2014
Class 42 B-B	Western	Heljan	2014
Class 45 1-Co-Co-1	Midland/Eastern	Heljan	2015
Class 52 'Western' C-C	Western	Heljan	2013
Class 60 Co-Co	All	Heljan	2014

Kernow Model Rail Centre's next 'OO' gauge release is the Adams 'O2' 0-4-4T.

2012 by seven from last year's 23 with increases in both steam and diesel circles.

The most dramatic news for 'N' gauge is the entry of DJ Models run by former Dapol Product Development Manager Dave Jones. To launch the business DJ Models has revealed it is planning models of the 'J94' 0-6-0ST, Class 17 and Class 23 for the scale alongside its plans for 'OO' and 'O' gauge.

Not to be forgotten is the announcement from Hornby that it is producing the 'Brighton Belle' 5-BEL EMU for 'N' as its first foray into the scale. Due for release in 2014 this model is already making rapid progress with the first pre-production samples shown in September.

The main competition for 'N' is between Bachmann's Graham Farish range and Dapol, both of which have substantial development plans for locomotives and rolling stock. Bachmann has 16 new locomotives planned – including new variants of the Class 37 and 47 – for release in the next 18 months.

In the diesel category Bachmann and Dapol have an equal number of planned models, but it is in the steam sector where Bachmann is leading the way. This has come about partly through the introduction of its coreless motor in the

The LBSCR Billinton 'H2' 4-4-2 has long been sought after as a ready-to-run model, and it will be available in 'OO' gauge in 2015 through Bachmann! 'Brighton Atlantic' 32421 South Foreland leaves Christchurch with the afternoon Bournemouth to Brighton train on July 16 1955.
David Hepburne-Scott/Rail Archive Stephenson.

The Midland '1F' 0-6-0T from Bachmann will be available with both open and closed cabs.

'WD' 2-8-0 in 2012 which has allowed smaller mechanisms with high power output to be produced. This has lead to an influx of new tank engine models.

The next arrival for steam from Bachmann is expected to be the Fairburn 2-6-4T which was expected in the *Hornby Magazine* office for review any day. On top of this the manufacturer has a healthy Midland theme to its steam models with products on the go including the 'Jinty' 0-6-0T, '4F' 0-6-0 and 'Duchess' 4-6-2.

While the Midland and Eastern have generally benefitted the most from the latest 'N' gauge models the Western and Southern also look set to have their turn. For the Western there are three new models in production – the '64XX' 0-6-0PT and 'Castle' 4-6-0 from Bachmann and the 'Grange' 4-6-0 from Dapol – while the Southern will see five new releases in the next 18 months. These include the Maunsell 'Schools' 4-4-0 from Dapol and the Maunsell 'N' 2-6-0 from Bachmann plus models of the air-smoothed 'Merchant Navy' 4-6-2 by Bachmann and both the air-smoothed and rebuilt 'West Country' 4-6-2 by Dapol.

'O' gauge

The growth in 'O' gauge ready-to-run is one of the most striking recent trends and this year it is racing ahead with 12 new locomotives planned by four manufacturers.

The market leader in British 'O' gauge ready-to-run is undoubtedly Heljan with its portfolio of diesel locomotives. Right now it is working on, or committed to producing, seven out of the 12 new locomotives for the scale! All are diesels and are due for release progressively from October 2013 through to the end of 2015.

Next in line from Heljan is the 'Western' diesel-hydraulic which was due to arrive in the UK in October. Following in the New Year it is planned that the Class 40 and then the AC Cars railbus will become available next.

Dapol's plans for the Class 08 and 'Terrier' 0-6-0T are also moving forward, but the 08 has stalled somewhat due to the quality of data available from the laser scan. However, both of these new – and affordable – locomotives are expected to be released in 2014. Plus Kernow Model Rail Centre's commission to Dapol for an 'O' gauge model of the delightful Beattie '0298' 2-4-0WT can't be forgotten.

The new name in model railways, DJ Models, also has plans for the scale with projects for a 'J94' 0-6-0ST and a Class 23 'Baby Deltic' announced at its launch in September 2013.

There is much more to come in 'O' gauge, particularly on the rolling stock front, and Dapol recently announced expansion plans for its 10ft wheelbase wagons while Heljan continues work on its BR Mk 1 parcels vans and BR freight wagons.

Overview

This hobby is incredible. The appetite for new locomotives seem to know no bounds, but what we have listed here is genuinely the tip of the iceberg. Add in the carriage and wagon models planned for production across the three scales and the list is more than impressive –it is becoming extremely comprehensive too.

Just a few years ago the majority of the models which are now becoming available ready-to-run were only available as kits and with today's production methods the quality of these products makes them better than the average man can make himself. Its an incredible, almost overwhelming, situation, and one which isn't without its risks. The affordability of such a large range of models has to be questioned and whether the market can really sustain such a massive influx of products.

The good news so far is that it can and has and naturally these products won't all appear overnight and more than likely some of those planned for release in 2014 will slip into 2015 making it easier for us, the customer, to spread the costs of the models we want over a longer period. It is an exciting time and each year the situation gets better and better and more towards the dreams we all have of complete collections.

We'll be keeping you posted on all these models and more in the pages of *Hornby Magazine* in the coming months plus don't forget to keep an eye out for our February dated issue which will come with a full 24 page preview to the Hornby range for 2014…

Heljan's 'O' gauge Class 40 is due for release in the first quarter of 2014.

HORNBY
magazine

The magazine for railway modellers of all ages

- Easy to follow 'How to' guides
- Superb photography, featuring some of the best layouts
- Historical and archive features to add realism to your layout
- STAFF PROJECTS – follow the editorial team at work

And much, much more...